D1085109

A. E. Housman Revisited

Twayne's English Authors Series

Kinley Roby, Editor
Northeastern University

TEAS 514

PORTRAIT OF A. E. HOUSMAN BY FRANCIS DODD
Courtesy of National Portrait Gallery.

A. E. Housman Revisited

Terence Allan Hoagwood

Texas A&M University

Twayne Publishers
An Imprint of Simon & Schuster Macmillan
New York

Prentice Hall International
London • Mexico City • New Delhi • Singapore • Sydney • Toronto

Twayne's English Authors Series No. 514

A. E. Housman Revisited
Terence Allan Hoagwood

Twayne Publishers
An Imprint of Simon & Schuster Macmillan
866 Third Avenue
New York, New York 10022

Library of Congress Cataloging-in-Publication Data

Hoagwood, Terence Allan, 1952-
  A. E. Housman revisited/by Terence Allan Hoagwood.
    p. cm.—(Twayne's English authors series; TEAS 514)
  Includes bibliographical references and index.
  ISBN 0-8057-7026-7
  1. Housman, A. E. (Alfred Edward), 1859–1936—Criticism and interpretation. I.
Title. II. Title: AE Housman revisited. III. Series.
PR4809.H15H56 1995
821'.912—dc20   95-2015
                                                                              CIP

10 9 8 7 6 5 4 3 2 1

Printed in the United States of America

Contents

Preface

To interpret a poem as a timeless classic is to conceal its meanings. All works of art—perhaps all products of human work—have meanings *in* and *of* their particular times and places. Timelessness is a sales pitch that defrauds its audience, and it also diminishes the meanings of works of art, concealing or denying the works' real-life engagements in their real-world settings. Because literary studies have been returning to an appreciation of historical and social meanings, and because Housman's poems have (and always had) historical meanings, some of which were and are controversial and even politically dangerous, the present may be a good time for a new assessment of Housman's thought and work.

In 1996, a century will have passed since the first publication of *A Shropshire Lad*. Housman's works and their meanings appear differently in that historical perspective from the ways in which they appeared during the intervening periods. Literary criticism sometimes looks disinterested in its aims, and its judgments sometimes sound permanent, but viewpoints are temporary. Conflicts come and go. Issues and values that seemed eternal, once, look obsolete fairly quickly, in historical terms.

The voice of Victorian religion in the nineteenth-century Church of England expressed certain judgments about Housman's work which will strike educated Americans in the 1990s as entirely foreign conceptions. In the period of the Boer War and again during World War I, Housman's poetry was used in connection with global political projects of which many educated readers in the 1990s know almost nothing. In his poems and his prose alike, Housman engaged in controversy with an intellectual movement, associated with F. R. Leavis (and the journal *Scrutiny*) and T. S. Eliot (and the journal *Criterion*), a movement whose political program involved a critique of modern industrialization and the degraded forms of commercialism associated with advertisement, which was even then becoming a way of life. To interpret Housman's poems as timeless is to erase these issues, to ignore and forget those meanings.

The illusory claim of timelessness has sometimes had some popularity in the past, because concentrated attention on meanings which are historically specific may seem to remove poems from us, and thereby to make them less valuable to us. The opposite is the case: the poems' real-world meanings and their special responses to their own temporary but actual world are what they have to say to us. The poems' truths are matters of their historical difference from us. It is precisely in their refraction of their world, consciously or unconsciously, that poems can teach us important things about ourselves. No poem is a perfect mirror; and the act of refracting (rather than merely reflecting) the imagery of a world is part of what we can learn from the study of poetry in general and from the study of Housman's work in particular.[1]

Housman's poetry has, in fact, been read and studied very widely indeed: as early as 1954, William White found that Housman's poems had already been included in 275 anthologies; in the 40 years since White's count, the number has been increasing continuously. Housman's readers and admirers have not all been scholars or students; from the publication of his first book onward, as Ghussan R. Greene has said, Housman's poems have been "read by many people who did not ordinarily read poetry": the poet John Masefield has told of "an old tramp" in whose pocket he found a copy of *A Shropshire Lad* which the tramp could quote precisely from memory. Beverly Nichols has told of "a meeting with a manufacturer of suspenders who, upon learning that Nichols was a writer, 'ran into the hall, got his bag and produced from a nest of suspenders a first edition of *A Shropshire Lad*, which he knew by heart.'" Housman apparently told his publisher, Grant Richards, about a visit from Clarence Darrow, who had wanted to meet Housman because "he had got off so many possible murderers by quoting poems out of *A Shropshire Lad* in support of his arguments.'"[2]

Apart from their popular appeal, Housman's poems have also received substantial attention from scholarly and critical authorities as well: books about Housman began to appear almost immediately after his death in 1936,[3] and of course good scholarly books about Housman's poetry continue to appear.[4] There have been scholarly controversies of considerable magnitude, including textual controversies associated with manuscripts in Housman's notebooks, involving matters of scholarly accuracy but also the question of the propriety of publishing poems that (according to the terms of his will) Housman had wanted his brother to destroy.[5] There have been controversies among biographers of Housman as evidence about his life has been interpreted differently,[6] and disputation is sometimes severe. Some of the most important writers and critics of the twentieth century have written about Housman, including T. S. Eliot, John Crowe Ransom, John Peale Bishop, Stephen Spender, Edmund Wilson, Cleanth Brooks, and others. The Housman Society, founded in 1973, has published an annual scholarly journal in which there have appeared scholarly essays, newly discovered writings of Housman and of members of his family, reviews of books about Housman, and (in some years) bibliographical essays by Benjamin Franklin Fisher IV listing and discussing scholarly and critical work on Housman. The publication in 1992 of an excellent collection of early reviews of Housman's poetry (to 1951) makes easily available the primary evidence of appreciations and arguments about Housman's work as they have developed and changed over time. The extent to which his poetry was itself involved in ideas and arguments (and not in sentimental or merely personal emotion) is easier to grasp now, in our own historical time and place, than it has been for many years past.

The present book includes commentaries on Housman's poems, including every one of the 63 poems in *A Shropshire Lad* and several from his other collections as well; but the book is written and organized to clarify, too, the connection of his life and work with his time (1859–1936) and his place (Bromsgrove, then Oxford, then London, and then Cambridge). Despite his nearly annual vacations to Europe, in the last few decades of his life, his place is always England—first Bromsgrove (which is in Worcestershire, *not* Shropshire), and then London, and then Cambridge; he writes sometimes of India or Africa, but always in connection with British imperial policy in those foreign lands. His learning (always) and his allusions (often) include ancient literature, history, and thought, but it is always in the context of England in the later nineteenth and earlier twentieth centuries that his meanings are to be found.

Though Housman is known now almost entirely for his poetry, his life's work was classical scholarship, and (by all available records) he never thought of *A Shropshire Lad* as the monument of his life's work; he thought that his monument was his edition, with extensive and detailed scholarly commentaries, of the work of Manilius, an ancient Latin author in whom few have been interested (ever), but on whom Housman worked for decades. I have tried not to forget, while writing this book about Housman the poet, that he was also one of the foremost classical scholars of his time, and one of the more important authorities on textual criticism.

In his most widely read and admired essay, "The Name and Nature of Poetry" (delivered as the Leslie Stephen Lecture at Cambridge University on 9 May 1933), Housman suggests about poetry in general, and his own poetry in particular, that intellectual content, in the sense of conscious, rational intentions of the author, often has little to do with the value of poetry *or* with the making of poetry. Housman suggests that powerful feelings from unconscious depths have much to do with the responses elicited by great poetry; conscious intention and logical content do not. I would point out, however, that Housman's making *that* argument was *itself* contentious: there was controversy about his lecture; he was understood at the time (1933) to be responding to the polemics of Leavis and *Scrutiny*. The argument that poetry is feeling rather than argument *is* an argument; the argument that poetry affects one personally rather than politically is *itself* made in a very public way, with an intent to affect the public. By design or otherwise—consciously, because of his ideas, or unconsciously, because he was unavoidably caught up in his historical time and place—Housman never stopped reacting to his world, and he never stopped framing its conflicts and its desires in the beautiful forms of his verse.

In chapter 1, I summarize facts about Housman's childhood and his intellectual life through his years at Oxford. As he knew well, the years of Housman's youth were years of explosive change in England's history, including intellectual developments and cultural changes of massive scale—for example, the rise of modern science; the increasingly obvious obsolescence of religious worship as it had been practiced institutionally for centuries; and the expansion of British imperialism and its wars. In chapter 2, I summarize facts about Housman's years in London, including his years of drudgery as a clerk in the Patent Office, studying ancient literature at night at the British Museum; his years as Professor of Latin at the University of London; and the writing and publication of *A Shropshire Lad*. In 1911, Housman accepted the appointment as Kennedy Professor of Latin at Cambridge University, and there he lived and wrote until his death in 1936, producing the monument of his classical scholarship, his admired essays ("The Confines of Criticism" and "The Name and Nature of Poetry"), and the only book of poems he published after *A Shropshire Lad*, which he aptly entitled *Last Poems*. This period in his life is the subject of chapter 3.

Throughout these three biographical chapters, I have discussed Housman's thought and writing in the context of his life: to separate his life in the world from his thought *about* it, and from his very thoughtful writings, would be a mistake.[7] After these chapters on his life and thought, chapter 4 presents a commentary (proceeding poem by poem) on *A Shropshire Lad*. This commentary discusses the question of the coherence and unity of the book as a whole, as well as details within individual poems. Chapter 5 discusses poems in *Last Poems, More Poems* (a collection of verse assembled by Laurence Housman after the poet's death), and (briefly) the set of other poems which Laurence culled from his brother's notebooks, entitled *Additional Poems*. The conclusion to this book is not a summary of its previous chapters, but an attempt to indicate the importance of Housman's thought and work.

Acknowledgments

From Reed Whittemore I learned how to think critically about how and why biographies are written; without Whittemore's books, conversation, and inspiration, I would not have written this book at all. Also formative on this book is what I have learned from Jerome J. McGann about two sorts of things: the importance of historical differentials, and the extent to which textual criticism is not merely a toolbox for editors but a way to think about the meanings of human work. The Housman Society has been an international community for the study and discussion of Housman; I am grateful specifically to John Pugh, Alan Holden, and Benjamin Franklin Fisher IV. For ten years, Hilary Hoagwood has talked helpfully with me about the poetry and prose of Housman, and the exchange of views has been influential in ways that this book's documentation cannot register adequately. Finally, I would like to acknowledge the good work of Anne Kiefer, editor of this book at Twayne: Ms. Kiefer's good judgment and editorial skill have improved the book.

For permission for the use of quotations from *The Collected Poems of A. E. Housman* (copyright 1965 by Holt, Rinehart and Winston), I thank Henry Holt and Company, Inc.

For the use of quotations from A. E. Housman's prose and letters and for the use of quotations from Katharine Symons and Laurence Housman, I acknowledge the Society of Authors as the literary representative of the Estate of A. E. Housman.

Francis Dodd's portrait of A. E. Housman is reproduced photographically for the frontispiece of this book, by courtesy of the National Portrait Gallery, London.

Chronology

1859 Alfred Edward Housman is born on March 26 in Fockbury, near Bromsgrove, in Worcestershire.

Charles Darwin's *The Origin of Species* is published.

1870 Housman wins a scholarship to King Edward's School (later called Bromsgrove School).

Suez Canal opens.

1871 Religious restrictions are removed at Oxford.

1876 Queen Victoria is declared Empress of India.

1877 Housman is awarded a scholarship to St. John's College, Oxford, where he goes in October to study classics.

A government of confederation is imposed by the British upon the Boers in southern Africa.

1878 Housman attends an anti-Russian demonstration at Oxford and writes to his father on 12 February about "the excited state of the public mind."

1879 The first colleges for women at Oxford are opened. In Africa, the British exterminate the Zulus.

1880–81 The first Boer War.

1881 Housman fails his exams at Oxford in May 1881 and returns home without a degree.

1882 Britain invades Egypt.

Housman returns to Oxford to take another exam and receives a "pass" degree.

In November Housman accepts a position as clerk in the Patent Office in London.

First scholarly publication, "Horatiana," appears in the *Journal of Philology*.

1885 The Labouchère Amendment of the Criminal Law Amendment Act makes all homosexual acts between men punishable.

1886   Gold is discovered in Transvaal, in southeastern Africa.

1887   British East Africa Company is formed and chartered by the British government.

1892   Housman is appointed Professor of Latin at University College, London.

1895   Macmillan rejects *A Shropshire Lad*.

Oscar Wilde is tried, convicted, and imprisoned for alleged homosexual acts.

1896   *A Shropshire Lad* is published by Kegan Paul.

1898   Grant Richards publishes a second edition of *A Shropshire Lad*; a third follows in 1898 and a fourth in 1902.

1899–1902   Second Boer War.

1901   Housman's brother Herbert dies in the Boer War.

1903   Housman publishes the first volume of his edition and commentary on Manilius's *Astronomica*. (Publishes the second book in 1912, the third in 1916, the fourth in 1920, and the fifth in 1930.)

1911   Appointed Kennedy Professor of Latin at the University of Cambridge, and Fellow of Trinity College, Cambridge. On 9 May delivers the Inaugural Lecture, later published as *The Confines of Criticism*.

1914   World War I begins, following assassination (in Sarajevo, Bosnia) of Archduke Ferdinand of Austria on 28 June. The British enter the war on 4 August.

1915   Housman grants permission for the printing of some of his poems in a collection of poetry to be supplied to soldiers in World War I.

1916   Bertrand Russell is convicted for antiwar activities, and is removed from his position as lecturer at Cambridge.

1918   World War I ends.

Women gain the right to vote in national elections in Britain.

1922   Housman publishes *Last Poems*.

1933   Delivers *The Name and Nature of Poetry* as the Leslie Stephen Lecture at Cambridge on 9 May.

1936   Gives his last lecture at Cambridge on 24 April and
        dies six days later.

        Laurence Housman assembles and publishes *More
        Poems*, a volume consisting of poems that Housman had
        left unpublished.

Chapter One

Housman's Childhood and Years at Oxford

Alfred Edward Housman was born 26 March 1859: in the same year appeared Charles Darwin's *On the Origin of Species*, one of the most influential books ever written to replace superstitions with scientific and naturalistic knowledge. That was also the year in which John Stuart Mill's *On Liberty* was published, one of the most eloquent arguments for political, intellectual, and moral freedom ever written in England. One of the great literary works of the year was George Eliot's *Adam Bede*, a novel that is in large part about historical changes taking place at the beginning of the nineteenth century and the economic, religious, and social conflicts that these changes involved.

Housman's birthplace and childhood were not situated in the thick of the intellectual and cultural turmoil, though he later became one of the foremost scholars and poets of his lifetime. Son of Edward Housman, a lawyer, and Sarah Jane Housman, née Williams, a clergyman's daughter, Housman was born in a small town, Fockbury, and his childhood home was in nearby Bromsgrove, Worcestershire, where his family moved during his infancy. Despite the misleading impression created by his most widely read book, *A Shropshire Lad*, Housman never spent much time in Shropshire, and though he sometimes used geographical names drawn from Shropshire, his local details are often, by his own admission, quite wrong.

In fact, Housman's poems are almost never autobiographical in the direct sense. His life and his times do help to determine his poetry's meanings, but not in the sense of autobiographical writing: the issues, emotions, and ideas in Housman's works are expressive of something far larger than his personality, which is in any case almost always concealed. Housman's works are expressive of the age in which he lived in more profound ways than writing about current events. Matthew Arnold, "his favorite English poet" in his Oxford years and later,[1] expresses in his poem "The Buried Life" what was also one of the central conditions of Housman's own life and work:

I knew the mass of men conceal'd
Their thoughts, for fear that if reveal'd
They would by other men be met
With blank indifference, or with blame reproved;
I knew they lived and moved
Trick'd in disguises, alien to the rest
Of men, and alien to themselves. . . .[2]

In his poetry and otherwise in his life, Housman does not openly express personal truths, but rather his art represents something very close to the opposite. It is only one obvious example that the author of *A Shropshire Lad* was no "lad," but Professor of Latin at University College, London (and 37 years old) when he produced that collection of poems. As the titles of books about Housman often recognize—for example, Percy Withers's *A Buried Life* (1940), and Maude Hawkins's *A. E. Housman: Man Behind a Mask* (1958)—buried truths are voiced through characters, through ironies, and despite suppression. Sometimes this suppression involves the burial of troublesome issues in symbolic forms, but sometimes it involves the outright suppression of works that Housman never published and which he ordered should be destroyed in manuscript.

Both of Housman's grandfathers had been clergymen, his maternal grandfather having been Rector of Woodchester; his paternal great-grandfather had also been a clergyman. Housman's parents were conservative in political and religious matters alike, and though Housman conformed outwardly with these customs during his childhood, his conformity did not last long. As he wrote much later, replying to a set of questions sent to him by Maurice Pollet, who was preparing to write a study of Housman: "I was brought up in the Church of England and in the High Church part, which is much the best religion I have ever come across. But Lemprière's Classical Dictionary, which fell into my hands when I was eight, attached my affections to paganism. I became a deist at thirteen and an atheist at twenty-one."[3]

Housman's father adhered to Tory (conservative) political positions, he belonged to the Bromsgrove Volunteer Rifle Corps, and after dinner he would sometimes assemble all seven of his children to shout his favorite political slogans before going to bed. In contrast, Housman later became one of the most skillful antiwar poets of the century. The family observed religious rituals with ceremonial rigor, including daily prayers before breakfast (in an enforced routine led by the father and including the servants), evening prayers, and attendance at church twice each Sunday. Housman became, as he said very plainly, an atheist.

In a family devoted to maintaining respectable appearances, Housman and his brothers and sisters were painfully aware of discrepancies between those outward appearances and the realities of their family life. His father reportedly became a heavy drinker, and his financial irregularities were so severe that he was repeatedly in legal trouble. Housman's father was, for example, once brought to court by his own mother, his brothers, and his sisters, for defrauding his father's estate, and once by an old family friend who had previously helped him out of serious financial problems.[4]

Housman's mother became seriously ill in 1869, with what proved to be breast cancer. She became more conservative in her religious preferences, reportedly asking to see a Roman Catholic priest in her illness. Her husband, still a staunch Anglican, refused. Housman, the oldest child, was frequently with her in her illness, praying with her and acquiring the belief that, if there were a God, she would recover. She did not recover. In March 1871, her illness growing worse, Housman was sent away against his wishes to stay for a while with some friends of the family, the Wises. Housman understood that his mother was seriously ill, and he did not want to go away from home. At the Wises' house, on his twelfth birthday (26 March 1871), he received a letter from his father reporting that his mother had died. His six brothers and sisters had been able to attend the funeral, though he had not. His father's letter also told Housman that his mother had specifically mentioned, while dying, her concern that Housman should not lose his religious faith.

In the meanwhile, Edward Housman was evidently drinking heavily during his wife's fatal illness, and he was involved in peculiar financial arrangements (which Richard Perceval Graves has explained in his biography). When Housman returned home from the Wises' house after his mother's funeral, he was responsible for keeping up appearances as well as helping to look after the younger children. As Norman Page has said, "from this period in his life dates the withdrawn, deeply reserved side of his nature that in later years was to grow dominant" (Page, 22). Housman's sister Katharine later said that the death of their mother deprived Housman "of a guide and counsellor who was never replaced. . . . From that time he became his own counsellor, confiding to no one his mental troubles or ambitions" (quoted in the introduction to Richards, xii, and in Page, 22). Housman later wrote that his loss of belief in a benevolent and providential god dated from about this time (*Letters*, 328).

Outwardly preserving religious ceremony and assertions, though belief in a benevolent god was gone, came to be an important feature of the sort of double life, with false surfaces and buried truths, that is represented in Housman's poetry as in much of the great literature of the Victorian period. Other circumstances of course contributed to that double life, some of them involving changes in the whole of British society and some being specific within Housman's family. In 1873, Edward Housman married his cousin Lucy, who thus became the children's stepmother and whom Housman's brother Laurence later described as "a tyrant . . . staunch to her duty as she saw it."[5] Housman and his siblings were taught that they should be ashamed if they were seen entering or leaving the bathroom. Laurence wrote that Lucy's regime brought about habits of "evasion and untruthfulness." The sense of a moral life in which the children were brought up was associated with habitual concealment; "one grew to feel that between the individual and the social environment was a barrier which had to be defended even from those whom one loved and might naturally have trusted."[6]

The strict maintenance of an outward appearance of moral propriety was a routine of traditional falsehood that the children knew well; for example, the behavior of Housman's paternal uncle Thomas had been notorious within the family since, as a boy, he was found leaving the bedroom of a woman servant (Graves 1979, 2), and late in his life Laurence Housman reported an incident in which as a child he was handled in an evidently sexual way by two respected household servants, though at the time he did not know what they wanted. Graves indicates that Housman reported to his stepmother some immoral behavior of a new governess which had disgusted him (but which Graves does not specify beyond using the word "promiscuity" [Graves 1979, 21 and 273 n]); the angry governess left the household while making insults about Housman's adequacy. While such events were kept secret, Lucy Housman reported proudly that "there were daily Bible readings in the family circle for many years."[7]

These two sets of issues on which duplicity and repression were enforced—religion and sexuality—were not merely personal experiences for Housman and his siblings; these issues involved important cultural crises for England and Europe throughout the nineteenth century, as Housman came to understand very well. Housman's poetry deals with these issues brilliantly, though never quite openly and directly. In

Housman's poetry, ironic language suppresses critical thought under an outwardly conventional and quiet surface.

From the age of 11, Housman attended King Edward's School (later called Bromsgrove School), having won a scholarship in 1870. He did very well in his studies, winning prizes, for example, for verse in Latin and Greek as well as English, and likewise for his ability in French. Socially he was troubled: because he was small, other boys stepped on him and called him "Mouse" (Symons, 8). There was also trouble at home: in the year before his mother's death, she called him more and more frequently to pray with her for her recovery. Her bed was moved to a position adjacent to the dining room, so that she could hear the family prayers too. As the oldest of the children, Housman apparently led the way in the suppression of personal feelings after the mother's death; the children never spoke of their loss. Religious rituals persisted, though Housman "secretly abandoned Christianity" (Graves 1979, 18).

In 1877, Housman was awarded a scholarship to St. John's College, Oxford, where he went (in October) to study classics. Housman's lifetime was a period of turbulent change at Oxford as in England generally.[8] Only in 1854 and then in 1856 were nonconformists (i.e., Protestants other than members of the Anglican Church) permitted to matriculate and take degrees at Oxford and Cambridge; members of any church other than the Anglican were not permitted to receive fellowships. Celibacy had been compulsory at St. John's College at Oxford until shortly before Housman's arrival. Only in 1871 were all religious restrictions removed at Oxford. The first colleges for women at Oxford were opened in 1879, during Housman's second year.

The content of the intellectual life was also undergoing conflict and change. Modern scholarship had been making important discoveries in biblical history and interpretation, for example, as in David Friedrich Strauss's *Life of Jesus* and in Ludwig Feuerbach's *Essence of Christianity*, of which George Eliot published English translations in 1846 and 1854. In 1860, Benjamin Jowett, an influential biblical and classical scholar and Regius Professor of Greek at Oxford since 1855, published an essay entitled "On the Interpretation of Scripture," in which he argued that the Bible could be studied using historical and textual methods of scholarship that were suitable for other ancient texts. The volume containing Jowett's essay was condemned by the church, and Jowett retreated from biblical studies (where his positions were forbidden) to classical scholarship and the study of Plato. According to Laurence Housman, Housman's "father would not allow him to try for a Balliol

6 A. E. HOUSMAN REVISITED

Scholarship from disapproval of the theological views of Dr. Jowett, the Master" (L. Housman 1938, 38).

Classical literature and philosophy were the predominant forms in which naturalistic, humanistic, skeptical, and atheist forms of thought were articulated in the years of intellectual repression. Scientists were still discovering (and struggling for freedom to express) the principles of natural science in biology, including cell structure in plants and animals, genetics and the evolution of species, and anatomy, including the study of the brain; geology, including the fact that the earth had changed according to natural laws for millions of years whereas there were still adults in England who believed that the earth had been created super-naturally six thousand years ago, complete with creatures just as they are found now; and other sciences, including molecular and atomic physics. Because the established church was (and had always been) a political institution in England, conservative resistance to these discoveries and their implications was severe. Housman was not evidently interested in the technicalities of science, saying candidly that "I never had any scientific education" (*Letters*, 328), though the man he called "my greatest friend," Moses Jackson, was an accomplished scientist. In Housman's view, however, the older religious explanations and beliefs were no longer relevant; in Housman's words, "it is up to Science to show what is the reality of the world."[9]

The history of ancient civilizations—Greek, Roman, and others—was an increasingly important preoccupation in the eighteenth and nineteenth centuries, as indicated, for example, by the founding of the British Museum in 1753 and its growth in the nineteenth century. Archaeology was as important in historical study as it was in geology. The old form of government-sponsored dogma (belief in the truth of the Bible) was being replaced by factual discoveries. Charles Lyell's *Principles of Geology* (1830–33) was the most influential work in replacing biblical with scientific understanding of the history and formation of the earth. Lyell's *Geological Evidences of the Antiquity of Man* (1863), like Darwin's *On the Origin of Species* and *The Descent of Man* (1871), used scientific evidence to show that the human species had evolved naturally over a much longer period of time than previously popular superstitions had allowed. Lyell's arguments involved what has been called "uniformitarianism"— the notion that the current conditions of the earth and of species are explicable by reference to "Causes Now in Operation" (in Lyell's phrase), and not by reference to a unique catastrophe in the past, such as Noah's flood. Robert Chambers (in his *Vestiges of the Natural History of Creation*

[1844]) expressed what has come to be called "catastrophism": species are mutable, and huge geological catastrophes bring about changes in the earth and among species, producing new animals of higher types. Chambers dismisses religious explanations and writes that "man, then, considered zoologically, and without regard to the distinct character assigned to him by theology, simply takes his place as the type of all types of the animal kingdom."[10]

The naturalistic view of the world—in terms provided by modern writers like Lyell and Chambers, no less than in terms provided by ancient writers including Lucretius—affected of course the entire cultural life of England, and not only its scientific community. Swinburne, whom Housman is said to have admired in his youth, writes (as Housman does after him) poems on the theme that "dead men rise up never," embodying emotions that follow from the recognition that after natural death there is "Only the sleep eternal / In an eternal night"; fantasies of heaven and hell are fruitless illusions:

> Though one were strong as seven,
> He too with death shall dwell,
> Nor wake with wings in heaven,
> Nor weep for pains in hell;
> Though one were fair as roses,
> His beauty clouds and closes;
> And well though love reposes,
> In the end it is not well.[11]

Swinburne's poetry suggests in its imagery (again as Housman's was to do after him) the naturalistic continuity of human beings with the rest of the material world. Swinburne uses the example of dead lovers, for example, which was to become a recurrent motif in *A Shropshire Lad*: "They are loveless now as the grass above them / Or the wave"; and "All are at one now, roses and lovers."[12]

The study of ancient peoples, like the study of biology and geology, also developed with archaeological methods, as evidenced by, for example, John Lubbock's book, *Pre-Historic Times*, which first divided the Paleolithic and Neolithic periods. The study of natural history coincided with the development of historiography, the study of ancient systems of ethics, and the study of classical and other ancient cultures. As knowledge of history increased—geological, biological, and cultural history alike—older, dogmatic beliefs weakened.

Housman had long been interested in these developments, though he remained without scholarly expertise in science: for example, "I took an interest in astronomy almost as early as I can remember" (*Letters*, 328), and his greatest work in classical studies, not completed until 1930, was his edition of an ancient work on astronomy, Manilius's *Astronomica*. When he was 15, he travelled to London, writing home to his stepmother (9 January 1875) of what he saw with special interest—not only the monuments of statesmen (and particularly William Pitt and Charles James Fox), but also exhibits at the British Museum. There he "spent most of my time among the Greeks and Romans"; he saw there his cousin Henry, whose conversation with Housman was "of course geological"; and he wrote of extinct species—the Mastodon, Megatherium, Echthyosauri, and Plesiosauri (*Letters*, 5–6). The topics discussed in what is apparently his first surviving letter—politics, statesmen, natural history, ancient Greece and Rome—are permanently important interests for Housman and his work.

What Housman studied at Oxford was not science, but rather classics, and within that subject matter he specialized not in the philosophical thought of the ancients (which was the form of study most recommended by Jowett) but rather what is called textual criticism. Many works of ancient literature whose original versions were lost have survived in different manuscripts made by later copyists. These different versions frequently disagree in content. Textual criticism is the scholarly endeavor to determine what exactly was the text of the lost original, on the basis of a careful comparison and critique of surviving versions. This scholarly work requires comprehensive knowledge of the ancient languages, literatures, customs, and culture, and it requires also a keen intellect and superior reasoning abilities. Though not until many years after he left Oxford, Housman was to become one of the foremost textual critics in the history of literature.[13] What he did at Oxford apparently included pursuing his studies in textual criticism of ancient poetry at the expense of other required studies, especially philosophy.

Among the educated population of England, it was widely understood that modern science, including evolution but not specifically the theory of natural selection, shared much with the moral and philosophical thought of ancient Greek and Latin writers. With or without the optimistic hypothesis of evolutionary progress (Housman never expresses such optimism), some general assumptions are common to classical materialism and modern science: the understanding that the earth and creatures alive upon it are material, that change happens according to natural phenomena and patterns rather than miraculous intervention of supernatural beings, that the life of a particular organism (including a human being) ends totally at death, that thought is a function of the material brain and not an invisible "soul," and that there are problems in articulating how life is morally meaningful in a world that may be made up of the random motion of atoms.

The great poetry of the later nineteenth century in England, including the poetry of Housman, frequently uses the artistry of classicism to express, indirectly, these ideas. While the implications of modern science met resistance and repression from hostile church authorities (who were also political authorities), and while advanced thought encountered bigotry widely among the frightened orthodoxy, Tennyson was able to explore the issues I have mentioned by way of ancient analogies, as in his poem "Lucretius." Matthew Arnold had done likewise in his poem, *Empedocles on Etna*.

In a lecture that was published in 1868, "On the Physical Basis of Life," Huxley summarized some of the more important implications of modern physical and biological science, including the fact that a common material is the substance of all living things. Protoplasm (i.e., protein) is the substance constituting all living beings. Living beings are made of the same sort of matter as other physical objects; the atoms are organized differently in the case of living beings, but they are matter just the same, and thought (no less than digestion) is a case of molecular change in this matter.

Ancient pagan philosophy had expressed a similar awareness about the physical basis of life, though without scientific detail: Lucretius writes, "I will reveal those *atoms* from which nature creates all things and increases and feeds them and into which, when they perish, nature resolves them. . . . the 'raw material,' or 'generative bodies,' or 'seeds' of things"; "for the same elements compose sky, sea and lands, rivers and sun, crops, trees and animals, but they are moving differently and in different combinations." Further, according to Lucretius *"The mind*, which we often call the intellect, the seat of the guidance and control of life, *is part of a man*, no less than hand or foot or eyes are parts of a whole living creature."[14]

The most recurrent issue in Housman's poetry is a shared feature of modern science and ancient philosophy: the problem of death, and of what becomes of a body (a person) after death. Lucretius presents a concept of continually recycled matter: "nature resolves everything into its component atoms and never reduces anything to nothing" (Lucretius, 33). And likewise, "You are withering [but] the old is always thrust aside to make way for the new, and one thing must be built out of the wreck of another. There is no murky pit of Hell awaiting anyone. There is need of matter, so that later generations may arise" (Lucretius, 125). Huxley emphasizes the ceaseless decay which occurs in living matter (and therefore among living creatures), and likewise he emphasizes the need for matter, for the formation of other living things.

Huxley, who coined the word "agnostic," did not insist dogmatically that there is no god, whereas Housman was emphatic about his atheism; what Huxley did was to show that certain old dogmas were untenable. Housman's skepticism was quite as trenchant as Huxley's, but Housman did not write didactic or doctrinal poetry insisting on opinions, atheistic or otherwise; like the poetry of Tennyson and Arnold, Housman's verse places the often melancholy vision of doubt and a world of perpetual dying in a form derived from ancient poetry, including Lucretius and many other poets. He writes with artistry and emotional depth but without dogmatism and in fact with some satirical treatment of dogmatism, conventional piety, and smug traditionalism. The burial of Housman's materialism and atheism under the lovely lyrical surface of his poems and under the minute and scholarly classicism of his professional writings is (like the wall of silence kept around the children's grief when their mother died, or like the mask of propriety concealing sexual abuses in the house) a sign of the historical times.

Housman's understanding of these issues—the shared conceptual ground of classical literature, modern science, and atheism—is evident from his writings, even from his undergraduate writings. At Oxford Housman wrote (in 1879) "Iona," a poem that he never published but which he entered in the competition for the Newdigate Prize for English poetry. In this poem, Housman denies immortality in language strikingly similar to Swinburne's "Garden of Proserpine," which I have quoted above: "These dusty dead shall speak no word again . . . these are dead & dust & done with quite."[15] Housman's poem is also similar to Swinburne's "Hymn to Proserpine" in its emphasis on the historicity of religions and superstitions, which pass away as people themselves do: "faiths & fanes & idols overthrown . . . dead." The fictitious speaker of Housman's poem has traveled to a mythically sacred island to find that it is in fact an "empty land"; he imagines many previous pilgrims having traveled to the same place in the distant past; but "now their gods &

they to us men seem / Vain, & thin air, & dimmer than a dream." The poem narrates the large historical change wherein superstitious faith was replaced by knowledge; because the truth that the poem treats is absolute mortality, people are portrayed as preferring their fantasies of immortality even after they have been shown to be unreasonable: "we will live our lives & die in dreams." Currently popular customs blind people to unwelcome truths: people are "blinded with the time's disease"; whatever superstition is dominant at a given time is said to deafen the people of that time to what the voice of truth is murmuring all the while: "While faith yet walks the waves, our hearing sleeps." On the supposedly sacred island, which is in fact a spot of empty earth, the poem's speaker reflects that soon the material ocean will "Strike cool on broken heart & fever'd brain"; in lines recalling Matthew Arnold's poem "To Marguerite" and analogous in conception with Huxley's essay "On the Physical Basis of Life," the poem's speaker says that over "brain & heart & hand shall be / Salt, & unsail'd, and islandless, the sea."

From the time that he first went to Oxford as an undergraduate, Housman was keenly aware of the constraints upon free expression. It is unwise to treat any poem by Housman, or any poem written during his lifetime, as if it were a trustworthy confession of true, personal feeling. Political power and enforced social codes prevented such sincerity. During his first Christmas vacation from Oxford, Housman wrote a short story in which a poet laureate writes of the queen tumbling "head over heels" into a ballroom; the king in the story objects to this unflattering description, and the poet laureate replies, "if you like I can alter it, and say she came into it heels over head. It wouldn't be true; but still, if you want me to, I'll say it."[16]

At Oxford, Housman attended at least one lecture by Jowett, reportedly expressing disgust at Jowett's interest in philosophical thought as opposed to linguistic and textual details.[17] He apparently attended college lectures on Plato, Aristotle, Herodotus, Cicero, Sallust, Tacitus, political philosophy, logic, Greek and Roman history, Bacon, Locke, Kant, and the utilitarians (Page, 36). He attended lectures by John Ruskin, one of the foremost authorities on the social and historical meanings of art, and he recorded in a letter the substance of what Ruskin said: "This afternoon Ruskin gave us a great outburst against modern times," displaying a picture by Turner of Leicester and the Abbey, over a river, and contrasting the landscape as it was in former centuries with the landscape now: "iron bridge . . . indigo factory . . . soap factory . . . red brick . . . smoke all over . . . and Ruskin confronting modern civilization amidst a tempest of applause" (*Letters*, 13). This set of issues also remained with Housman, who was to write many years later, with some bitterness, of the modern degradation of previously beautiful landscapes (see, for example, *Letters*, 30–31).

Housman's interest in political issues has never received much serious attention, but he expressed those interests early and unmistakably. During his first year at Oxford, he wrote to his father about debates at the Oxford Union: in 1876, Bosnia, then a province of Turkey, revolted, and other conflicts erupted in the region, including "the systematic murder of 12,000 Bulgarian men, women, and children by Turkish troops."[18] Disraeli, the Prime Minister, did not apparently view these atrocities as cause for British action; Gladstone, who had been Prime Minister until 1875, was a leader of the popular movement in England calling for humanitarian relief for those people who were suffering atrocities at the hands of the Turks, but when Russia declared war on Turkey, Disraeli supported Queen Victoria's decision to wage war against Russia. War against Russia was evidently aid to Turkey, and the liberals led by Gladstone responded with vigorous moral and political protest. On 12 February 1878 Housman writes to his father that Gladstone had spoken at Oxford some days before, and that "owing to the excited state of the public mind, the attendance at the debate was tremendous" (*Letters*, 14). Housman personally attended an anti-Russian demonstration and wrote at length to his (conservative) father about the conflict, from a conservative point of view (*Letters*, 13–19). On this issue overt repression took place: at Oxford "the Vice-Chancellor announce[d] that any undergraduate who should take part in any political meeting would be fined. . . . All the nights there have been crowds of both parties promenading the streets and singing" political songs (*Letters*, 20).

In his second year, he passed the required examinations (consisting chiefly of exercises in translation), earning an evaluation of first class. In 1880, Housman moved his residence out of college buildings to share rooms with two other undergraduates, A. W. Pollard and Moses Jackson. Page has called Housman's relationship with Jackson "the love affair of his life" (Page, 41), and Haber writes that Housman's admiration for Jackson "grew into affection 'passing the love of women'" and that "he became trammeled in a net of emotional complexes from which he could not extricate himself" (Haber 1967, 47). More temperately, Housman's brother Laurence writes that Housman's "deepest friendships were with men, that those friendships caused him trouble and grief, and that—in one instance at least (i.e., his friendship with Moses Jackson)—he gave a far greater devotion than he ever received in return."[19] Page quotes a letter from Laurence Housman to Maude Hawkins, who was preparing a biography of Housman, indicating his certainty that a few years later Housman "was in closer and warmer physical relationship" with Moses Jackson's brother, Adalbert, than with Moses.[20]

In the male communities of the ancient universities, Oxford and Cambridge, relationships of deep affection between men were nurtured. Tennyson's *In Memoriam* (1850), an elegy for Arthur Henry Hallam, the poet's friend from his days at Cambridge, is one of the most widely read expressions of the love of a friend. Until 1869, there was no concept of "a homosexual,"[21] though certain acts were forbidden. In England sodomy had been a crime punishable by death since 1533, and remained punishable by death until 1861. In the first three decades of the nineteenth century, according to Louis Crompton, 80 men were hanged for sodomy. Far larger numbers were punished in another way: if a man was found guilty of inviting or attempting sodomy, but completion of the act of sodomy could not be proved, he could be sentenced to the pillory, where he would be pelted by angry mobs under the supervision of the police. Under these severe conditions, homosexual feelings as well as homosexual practices were concealed: the novelist William Beckford fled from England, apparently in danger because of his homosexual tendencies, and Lord Castlereagh, British foreign minister, committed suicide when he was blackmailed in connection with his homosexuality.[22] Later in the nineteenth century, and well after Housman's Oxford years, the legal and political problems were still severe: in 1885, a new law (the Labouchère Amendment of the Criminal Law Amendment Act) made *all* homosexual acts between men punishable, and not only sodomy, as previously (Page, 55–56).

In England, obviously, homosexuality was covert, but it was also notorious: in 1889, the Cleveland Street scandal involved the discovery and publicizing of a male brothel. In 1895 Oscar Wilde, important poet, playwright, and novelist, was tried, convicted, and imprisoned for homosexuality. Late in the nineteenth century, and in the twentieth, some writers—including John Addington Symonds, Edward Carpenter, and Havelock Ellis—published studies on the issue of homosexuality and argued against the continued brutality of its repression in modern England, but "the courts ordered the first English scientific text on homosexuality destroyed shortly after its appearance in 1898" (Crompton, 4). Housman's brother Laurence became chairman of the British Society for the Study of Sex Psychology, which had been established in 1914, and he published the text of a 1916 lecture, "The Relation of Fellow-Feeling to Sex," as number four in a series of pamphlets published by that Society.[23] After Housman's death, Laurence indicated that Housman had never spoken to him of his homosexuality, but that he believed that Housman knew that Laurence understood it, and that Housman fully expected Laurence to publish (after Housman's death) poems more directly expressive of problems connected with his feelings of male friendship than any poems that Housman had himself published (L. Housman 1976, 20).

Whether or not Housman's relationship with Jackson involved homosexual feelings, his last year at Oxford included severe difficulties of other kinds. Six days before the final set of examinations required of Oxford undergraduates, Housman learned that his father (who had not been earning enough money to support the family or to make payments on mortgages that he held) was seriously ill. Housman failed his exams in May 1881, and had to return home without a degree. Reasons that have been suggested for his failure include his neglect of the required studies at Oxford (chiefly philosophical studies) in favor of his preferred study of textual details (especially study of the texts of Propertius). Whether emotional turbulence connected with his friendship with Jackson was related to his academic failure, or whether he was distracted by anxiety about his father's serious health problem or his family's financial problems must remain conjectural. Beyond the obvious reasons for concealment of certain parts of his life, his sister Katharine later wrote that Housman "very much lived in water-tight compartments that were not to communicate with each other."[24]

Chapter Two
Housman's Years in London

The Patent Office and the British Museum

At Bromsgrove, Housman was offered occasional teaching at the school where he had been a student. He studied so that he could return to Oxford to take another exam, and in 1882 he did so, though the degree that he received (a "pass") was inferior to what had been expected of him. In June 1882 he passed the Civil Service exam to qualify himself for employment, and in November 1882 he accepted a position as clerk in the Patent Office in London, where Moses Jackson also worked. He shared rooms with Moses and Adalbert Jackson for three years. A silence of five years intervenes between Housman's letter of 10 May 1880 to his stepmother, from Oxford (about undergraduates participating in political demonstrations) and the next published letter, 29 March 1885, also to his stepmother, from Housman's residence in Bayswater. Henry Maas, editor of Housman's letters, says that the intervening years were "the unhappiest time of Housman's life." These years, of course, include his failure at Oxford, his taking a lower degree, his father's illness, his family's financial problems, and his own taking the job as clerk in the Patent Office. Maas also indicates, however, that he has not been permitted to reproduce Housman's letters to Moses Jackson and a few other letters as well. Referring both to Housman's homosexual feelings and also his atheism, Maas writes that "at heart he defied the world" though "outwardly [Housman] preserved an appearance of rigid propriety" (*Letters*, 22 n).

It would be a mistake to interpret the meaning of Housman's suppression of his own attitudes, and the conventional constraint imposed on his public utterances, in terms of anything so small as his personal sexual proclivities: it is true that sodomy had been a capital crime until two years after Housman's birth, and that persons known to him (including Oscar Wilde) were imprisoned for allegedly indecent (homosexual) behavior; when Wilde was released from prison, Housman sent him a copy of *A Shropshire Lad*, and Wilde later praised the poetry in a letter to Laurence Housman.[1] Other and larger issues, however, required suppression in Victorian England. For example, Laurence Housman suffered censorship of many of his plays on political grounds; government controlled what political and religious attitudes were permissibly expressed.[2] As John Pugh has written, "Laurence had thirty-two of his plays censored, and there was not one indecent line in any of them" (Pugh, 170). In the conduct of his personal and social life and likewise in the content of his published work, Housman was constrained to suppress certain sexual subjects, but he was also constrained to suppress (by silence, or by indirect expression through irony, or through classical symbolism) other important subjects, including his hostility to imperialistic war and his atheism.

In May 1885 Housman writes cheerfully to his stepmother, joking about his work in the Patent Office and even about religious matters: "An elaborate new Index of Trade Marks is being compiled at the Office. It goes on very remarkable principles which I do not quite understand. Under the head of 'Biblical Subjects' is included an old monk drinking out of a tankard; and the Virgin Mary and St. John the Baptist are put among 'Mythical Figures'" (Letters, 24). In June 1885 Housman writes to his stepmother about politics ("Civil Servants in these days of course live in hourly expectation of being blown up by dynamite for political reasons"), suicide (Housman had served on a Coroner's jury that rendered a judgment about "one laundryman who tied a hundred-weight to his neck and tipped over into the water-butt; one butcher's man who cut his throat with a rusty knife"), and other matters (Letters, 25).

While working at the Patent Office, Housman also continued his scholarly study by reading in the evenings at the British Museum. The character of Housman's divided life is eloquently represented by Alan Ker: "On going down from Oxford he entered . . . H. M. Patent Office, where he is said to have been the worst clerk they ever had. But he was engaged in more important business, papers for the Journal of Philology on the Greek tragedians and on Horace and Propertius. Already in less than ten years he was the obvious choice for the chair of Latin at London University, and in nineteen more he was the only man in England worthy to succeed Munro in the Kennedy Professorship at Cambridge" (Symons, 49).

His first scholarly publication appeared in 1882, an article entitled "Horatiana" in the Journal of Philology. In 1883, he published an article on Ovid. For a few years, while he lived with Moses and Adalbert Jackson, Housman published nothing, as Page points out. In 1885, he moved out of the lodgings that he had shared with Moses and Adalbert

Jackson, and it was also in 1885 that he proposed to Macmillan his scholarly edition of Propertius. That publisher rejected the proposal, and the work was never published, reportedly having been destroyed after Housman's death; Housman's emendations, however—the changes in the received text for which he produced arguments—were published in the *Journal of Philology* in 1888. Though he had published nothing between 1883 and 1887, in that year he resumed publishing learned articles, and he continued publishing at an impressive rate for the rest of his life.

At the Patent Office, some of Housman's colleagues did not even know of his scholarly interest,[3] but during his 10 years there he published 25 scholarly articles. In 1892, having achieved an international reputation as an outstanding classical scholar, he applied for the position of Professor of Latin at University College, London. With his letter of application he sent 17 testimonials of his excellence as a classical scholar from many of the foremost scholarly authorities in the world.

Professor of Latin, University College

An Introductory Lecture from a professor in the college was delivered at the beginning of each academic year at University College, and as the new Professor of Latin, Housman was invited to deliver one in 1892. His thoughtful and beautifully written lecture was subsequently printed by the Council of University College, and it was apparently the only one in this series ever to have received that honor (John Carter, note to "Introductory Lecture," [*Prose*, 1]). In this lecture, Housman joins the debate that had been taking place in England for many years about the purposes and value of knowledge, higher education, and, specifically, classical education. Other great Victorians who had treated these issues, and to whom Housman responds, explicitly or implicitly, include John Henry Newman, Matthew Arnold, Thomas Henry Huxley, and Herbert Spencer.

With great clarity and wit, Housman states and rejects the two most popular views—the view that scientific study is valuable for its practical usefulness, and the humanists' view that study of the classics can transform and beautify one's inner nature. Instead, Housman argues that the most widely stated views "are the fabrications of men anxious to impose their own favourite pursuits on others," or the inventions of people who are uneasy until they can point to an external justification for their favorite activities (*Prose*, 16). He admits that the pursuit of truth does not always produce happiness: "it may be urged on the contrary that the pursuit of truth in some directions is even injurious to happiness, because it compels us to take leave of delusions which were pleasant while they lasted" (*Prose*, 19). Some pleasant delusions are religious beliefs, which many had found comforting for centuries, but on which light was being shed by the pursuit of truth, which would rob those delusions of their power. Housman argues that "the desire of knowledge does not need, nor could it possibly possess, any higher or more authentic sanction than the happiness which attends its gratification" (*Prose*, 17). He admits that not everyone will be able to appreciate all pleasures—"we see, every day of our lives . . . people, as Plato agreeably puts it, who wallow in ignorance with the complacency of a brutal hog" (*Prose*, 17); but for minds with the freedom and capability to experience the desire for knowledge and the delight of its satisfactions, "the tree of knowledge will remain for ever, as it was in the beginning, a tree to be desired to make one wise" (*Prose*, 22).

The thoughts expressed in this essay remain important for Housman, with impressive consistency, for all of his adult life. From his undergraduate poems, including especially "Iona," to one of his final statements of his ethical views (the letter to Maurice Pollet), it is the intrinsic goodness of happiness (pleasure, defined broadly) and not obedience to an abstract or inhuman code of rules that Housman values most. Late in his life, he writes thus to Pollet: "I respect the Epicureans more than the Stoics, but I am myself a Cyrenaic" (*Letters*, 329). The Epicureans were ancient philosophers who argued that pleasure is the greatest good for human life, and that intellectual pleasures were the greatest; the Stoics were ancient philosophers who argued that submission to one's lot in life was required, pleasure or no pleasure, on the assumption that a universal power of reason had somehow organized all things; but the Cyrenaics, with whom Housman expresses closest affinity, agreed with the Epicureans that pleasure was the greatest good. The Cyrenaics differed from the Epicureans in valuing different pleasures (including sensory pleasures) according to their intensity rather than their intellectuality.

On a more specific issue, too, the Introductory Lecture states a position about which Housman is remarkably consistent for the rest of his life: that is his contempt for a life dominated by concern for money. In the lecture he ridicules Herbert Spencer's contention that the worth of sciences is the extent to which they "render one efficient in producing, preparing or distributing commodities" (*Prose*, 4). The material necessities of life, Housman points out, do not in themselves amount to happiness, or assure happiness; "a life spent, however victoriously, in securing the necessaries of life is no more than an elaborate furnishing and decoration of apartments for the reception of a guest who is never to come" (*Prose*, 7). Housman's life and work were consistently devoted to other concerns than money: for example, he repeatedly made decisions about the publication of his poetry without regard to obtaining any profit for himself. He wrote in 1898 to the publisher of the second edition of *A Shropshire Lad*: "I do not want any profits" (*Letters*, 49). Many years later, in 1924, he refused to accept payment from the proceeds of a French translation of *A Shropshire Lad* (*Letters*, 218). Housman had other and better reasons for his work, as, in the Introductory Lecture, he argues that all persons require other and better reasons than profit or the acquisition of material goods.

Housman remained as Professor of Latin at University College for 19 years, during which he was very busily devoted to his work: for most of his years there, he was the *only* faculty member in Latin at that College, though in the last few years he had "the part-time assistance of a junior colleague" (Page, 64). University College had been founded in 1828 as a progressive alternative to the ancient universities; women were admitted, science was taught, and there were no religious requirements for admission (see Graves 1979, 82). Housman worked assiduously, and for some of his years at University College he served as Dean of Arts and Laws.

Housman was an active member of the College Literary Society, where he presented papers on Arnold, Burns, Campbell, Erasmus, Darwin, Swinburne, Tennyson, and the "Spasmodic School."[4] R. W. Chambers, who had been a student at University College when Housman was a Professor there, writes of a paper by Housman about Arnold, in which Housman disparaged Tennyson in comparison: "he described the argument of *In Memoriam* as being that 'things must come right in the end, because it would be so very unpleasant if they did not'" (Symons, 43). This ridicule of believing that something is true because one wishes it were true is entirely consistent with the tone of many of Housman's poems, in which poems' speakers refuse the illusory consolations of wish fulfillment; for example, in *More Poems* XLIII the speaker does not hallucinate about a happy heaven in (or beyond) the sky but sees only the actual "empty moors of air"; and rather than express conventional sentimental fantasies of progress or redemption, the poem's speaker concludes, "And on through night to morning / The world runs ruinward."

Chambers also reports an incident illustrating how careful Housman was about the publication of his work—including the prevention of the publication of work that he did not want to be printed, for whatever reason:

> Housman differed from his colleague Platt [Professor of Greek at University College, London] in the care he took that his papers, read before colleagues and students, should not be printed. He gave one of the earliest of the Foundation Orations of University College Union Society, a discourse which sparkled with all his accustomed wit. It is the habit to print these Orations. We noticed, as Housman went on, that he continued tearing up little bits of paper; we noticed it because such nervous fidgetiness was unlike him. When the President at the end made the usual request for the manuscript, Housman replied that it had been destroyed. As the address proceeded, he had been tearing up each page of his discourse after the other. (Symons, 45)

Housman never represented himself as a literary critic; he repeatedly avoided writing and publishing literary criticism, and he disparaged his own aptitude for it. He represented his life's work as classical scholarship, not literary criticism. By the time he left University College to become Kennedy Professor of Latin at Cambridge, Housman had published 99 classical papers, the first volume of his edition of Manilius, an edition of Juvenal, and an edition of Ovid's *Ibis*. The importance and excellence of Housman's work are indicated by Alan Ker, who called Housman "the greatest Latin scholar of his generation": besides his commentary and edition of Manilius and his editions of Juvenal (1905) and Lucan (1926), "he did as much as any contemporary scholar (and in most cases more) for the text of Lucilius, Persius, Lucretius, Horace, Propertius, Ovid, Martial, Statius, and the minor Latin Poets; and in Greek he showed the same skill in emending some of the new papyrus fragments" (Symons, 49, 53). A. S. F. Gow writes that Housman's classical scholarship "showed not only a mind of unusual penetration, but also so complete mastery of the technique of scholarship that the work of other scholars tended, beside his, to look amateurish" (Symons, 55).

While Housman was industriously and successfully establishing a professional life, it does not appear that his personal life was equally happy. In 1887, Moses Jackson had left for India, to take up the position of Principal of Sind College in Karachi. Housman wrote letters to him that were apparently unanswered. He saw Jackson in 1889, when the latter returned to England to marry Rosa Chambers. Housman was not invited to the wedding, and he heard later from others that Jackson had returned with his wife to India. Some verses that Housman never published may or may not be attempts to develop poetry from feelings suggested by this personal episode, though in any case he never published the poems. For example, *More Poems* XXXI begins,

> Because I liked you better
> Than suits a man to say,
> It irked you, and I promised
> To throw the thought away.

But what may or may not be an expression of homosexual feeling is quickly subordinated to the poem's larger theme: the imagined man whom the poem's speaker had liked more than he could suitably say dies and in death is said (in the final stanza) utterly and permanently to forget.

Again, the second poem in the series that (after Housman's death) Laurence Housman published as *Additional Poems* may or may not have taken its start from reflections on the broken friendship or love for Jackson. The poem begins, "Oh were he and I together"; the speaker imagines their sailing to France or Spain and their "Locking hands" on a battlefield; but its last stanza begins, "Now are he and I asunder," emphasizing not personal love but rather imperial wars ("Kingdoms are for others' plunder") and mortality ("And content for other slain").

Other sources of sadness and distress accumulated during the first years of the professorship he had struggled for a decade to earn. In 1892, Adalbert Jackson died, and *More Poems* XLII, entitled "A. J. J.," is apparently about the poet's dead friend, at least on the poem's literal level. From the first stanza, however, the poem is about something more important than any single person's grief: the dead are said never to hear, or to care, or to return, or to live again in any form.

In 1894, Housman's father died of heart failure, having suffered ill health for some time, including a stroke in 1881; Graves writes that "it was well known that he drank too much and worked far too little"; and in a poem said to be a "personal tribute to his father," Housman wrote, "The thirst that rivers could not lay / A little dust has quenched for aye" (*Additional Poems* XI A—see Graves 1979, 128–29). Housman's sister Katharine later wrote that at his father's death Housman "did not feel grief, beyond the inevitable poignant memories of youth" (Graves 1979, 102).

In the months after his father's death, which were coincidentally also the months of Oscar Wilde's trial and sentencing, Housman wrote poetry in what he later called "my most prolific period, the first five months of 1895"; but Housman, who did not speak highly of his own poetry, associated his poetic productivity with a "sore throat," indicating that his poetry "sprang chiefly from physical conditions" (*Letters*, 329). During that period of the sore throat, the death of his father, and Wilde's conviction, Housman wrote most of the poems that were published in 1896 in one of the great poetic books of the nineteenth century, *A Shropshire Lad*. Here is Housman's description of how he wrote (or at least began) some of the poems in that book: "Having drunk a pint of beer at luncheon—beer is a sedative to the brain, and my afternoons are the least intellectual portion of my life—I would go out for a walk of two or three hours. As I went along, thinking of nothing in particular, only looking at things around me and following the progress of the seasons, there would flow into my mind, with sudden and unaccountable emotion, sometimes a line or two of verse, sometimes a whole stanza at once" ("The Name and Nature of Poetry," in *Prose*, 194).

Sometimes stanzas would come to him with similar ease on other days to help to complete a poem, "but sometimes the poem had to be taken in hand and completed by the brain, which was apt to be a matter of trouble and anxiety." Housman tells that the poem that appears last in *A Shropshire Lad* (a poem that is 16 lines in length) took an entire year to finish, and that it had to be rewritten 13 times.

Housman had apparently intended to entitle the book *Poems of Terence Hearsay* (A. W. Pollard, in Symons, 33): in contrast to the poet, this character was to be a young man from Shropshire, and speeches and songs from his point of view (not Housman's) would provide the narrative framework for the collection. Originally, Housman intended to publish the book without his own name at all. Housman's friend from his undergraduate years, A. W. Pollard, suggested that a better title would be *A Shropshire Lad*, and Housman evidently agreed. After Macmillan rejected the proposed book in 1895, Housman arranged its publication, at his own expense, with Kegan Paul, in 1896. Published reviews of the book were favorable, but the book's sales were modest at first. Another publisher, Grant Richards, took over the volume and published a second edition in 1898; a third edition appeared in 1900; a fourth edition appeared in 1902; and composers (including Ralph Vaughan Williams) set some of the poems to music.[5] A pocket edition was produced in 1904 (*Letters*, 49 n). Numerous editions continued to be produced in England and in

America as well. Sales grew, especially after the 1906 edition. He became more and more highly regarded, and more and more popular as a poet; still, he viewed classical scholarship (and not poetry) as his life's work.

The elegant simplicity of the diction of Housman's poems masks the profound conflicts with which the poetry deals. The first poem in the book, for example, "1887," pretends to praise Queen Victoria in celebration of the fiftieth anniversary of her coming to the throne ("God save the Queen"); but the superficial tone of praise covers bitter satire of the massive bloodshed caused by imperial wars: of the soldiers whom the queen sent to die in imperial wars, the poem says, "Themselves they could not save." Many of the poems are similarly vigorous in their anti-war sentiment, but their lovely surfaces and often ironic speakers have so totally taken in some readers that Housman has sometimes been mistaken for a patriotic poet celebrating the virtues of a soldier's life, rather than (as he was) a skeptic voicing grief and anger at brutality, suffering, and conventional hypocrisy. In fact, Housman reports with some ridicule that the manager of Kegan Paul, first publisher of *A Shropshire Lad*, "was particularly captivated with the military element; so much so that he wanted me at first to make the whole affair . . . into a romance of enlistment" (*Letters*, 36). Housman refused. The patriotic sales pitch flatly contradicted the meanings of the poems, especially those that attack with irony the recruitment and enlistment of ignorant youth who die in hypocritically justified wars of imperialistic conquest (e.g., poem III, "The Recruit," or IV, "Reveille").

Other controversial issues are also dealt with, sometimes in slightly veiled ways. Laurence Housman writes that he found, in Housman's personal copy of *A Shropshire Lad*, a newspaper article from 6 August 1895, reporting the suicide of a Woolwich cadet at the age of 18. The article, which Laurence Housman found beside poem XLIV ("Shot? so quick, so clean an ending?"),[6] included quotations from the letter that the young man had left to explain his suicide to the coroner. Apparently the young man's shame and fear about his homosexuality prompted the suicide, and as Laurence Housman says, "it is quite evident that certain passages in that letter prompted the writing of the poem" (L. Housman 1938, 103–104; and see Graves 1979, 104). Housman's poem suggests, bitterly, that so much suffering would predictably have been inflicted on the young man through bigotry and hatred that his suicide was "wise and brave" (stanza 1). Other poems in the volume are about suicide (for example, poem XVI). Some poems are equally explicit about "Horror and scorn and hate and fear and indignation" (poem XLVIII), endowing with greater urgency the emotional conflicts as of "ice and fire" that many have felt when "Fear contended with desire" (XXX).

Ethical urgencies, too, are intensified by the conflicts, danger, anger, and desire that recur in poem after poem so that sometimes very simple sentences acquire in their context great poignancy and intensity of feeling: lives are fragile and short, death is final and meaningless, and a moral imperative emerges from that recognition in desperation and integrity: "Take my hand quick and tell me, / What have you in your heart" (XXXII). The final stanza of the poem on the suicide (XLIV) says that to die is to "Turn safe to rest, no dreams, no waking"—bodily death is the final end, and immortality is denied. What remains after a brief life in *A Shropshire Lad*, after "this fire of sense decay[s]," is no immortal soul, and no personal identity at all, but only "ancient night alone" and "The steadfast and enduring bone" (XLIII).

In Housman's poetry, that notion is not a doctrine, not an argument, but a felt awareness whose emotional power is one of the recurrent themes of the book. One does not often turn to Housman's poetry for philosophical originality, and he says later, very plainly, that poetry is not primarily intellectual, but that it deals with levels of experience more profound than superficial, conscious, rational thought—the power of poetry, Housman says, is emotional and even physical. (That point is one of the central contentions of Housman's lecture, "The Name and Nature of Poetry.") The patterns of thought and structures of feeling that most frequently characterize Housman's poems are in fact classical—skepticism about philosophical matters, refusal and ridicule of comforting illusions (like religion and superstition of all kinds), recognition of the natural mortality of every person, the brevity of life, and the urgency of kindness and happiness, made more intense by honest consciousness of mortality.

Stylistically, Housman's poems have suggested to many readers their analogies with classical poetry, owing to their virtues of elegance, simplicity, clarity, and compression. Conceptually, too, as I have suggested, Housman's poems share much with classical poets, especially in terms of atheism and Epicurean (or Cyrenaic) ethics. Housman indicated that he had read the Greek lyrics of love, delight, death, melancholy, and joy that were gathered in the widely read collection known as the Greek Anthology; he responded to Pollet's inquiry about the influence of that work on his poetry in this way: "'Reader of the Greek Anthology' is not a good name for me. Of course I have read it, or as much of it as is worth reading, but with no special heed" (*Letters*, 328). It is worth considering

for a moment his mixed response to this work because it reveals a great
deal about his poetry and thought, not only in *A Shropshire Lad*, but
throughout his long and varied career as scholar and writer.

One short poem from the Greek Anthology, a translation from
Simonides entitled "Uncertainty of Life," expresses very clearly the
classical (skeptical and Epicurean) themes that Housman develops
characteristically in *A Shropshire Lad* and elsewhere. It also shows, by
contrast, what distinguishes Housman's poems from so many others
that had been written on analogous themes for many centuries: whereas Housman's poems, short as they are, represent vividly particular
(imaginary) persons in concrete situations, imagining intensities of
feeling in specifically realized moments, the tendency of Simonides'
poem (and many others in the collection) is to leave the issues at
abstract or generalized levels:

> All human things are subject to decay;
> And well the man of Chios turned his lay,
> 'Like leaves on trees the race of man is found.'
> Yet few receive the melancholy sound,
> Or in their breasts imprint this solemn truth;
> For hope is near to all, but most to youth.
> Hope's vernal season leads the laughing hours,
> And strews o'er every path the fairest flowers.
> To cloud the scene no distant mists appear,
> Age moves no thought, and death awakes no fear.
> Ah, how unmindful is the giddy crowd
> Of the small span to youth and life allow'd.
> Ye who reflect, the short-lived good employ,
> And while the power remains, indulge your joy.[7]

The "unmindful . . . crowd" reappear as "the careless people" in *A
Shropshire Lad* XIV; the lament about "the small span to youth and life
allow'd" is transformed into the much more specific story of a man's
emotionally charged memory of his dead friend:

> Smart lad, to slip betimes away
> From fields where glory does not stay

> And early though the laurel grows
> It withers quicker than the rose.

To mention only one more example of Housman's more precisely imagined treatment of these themes, the final poem of *A Shropshire Lad*, LXIII, refers to the poems in the collection under the metaphor of flowers, which the poem's speaker says he has carried to the fair, but which were there "unheeded" because their color was not what was then most in demand; he has now scattered them:

> Some seed the birds devour,
> And some the season mars,
> But here and there will flower
> The solitary stars. . . .

What is merely generalized as "short-lived good" or "joy" in the Greek Anthology's sample from Simonides is here made visual (flower, star, birds), but the solitary moments of beauty under the condition of relentless loss led on in the movement of seasons is (again, conceptually) very similar. Housman's poems bear comparison with earlier English poetry on the same themes (frequently identified by a phrase from the Latin poet Horace, *carpe diem*), but such comparison is most rewarding when it reveals the distinctiveness of Housman's treatment. That distinctiveness involves Housman's placement of the classical themes in the contemporary (late nineteenth-century) context in two ways: his antiwar poetry locates the laments on death and the moral (Epicurean) urgencies in a specific historical time and place, when England's imperialism and imperial wars were expanding and intensifying. Further, Housman's presentations of atheism and naturalism acquire added meaning when they are understood in the context of late nineteenth-century England, when modern science was more and more rapidly removing the superstitious illusions that had governed the lives of previous generations.

Among ancient Latin poets, Housman's favorite was apparently Horace. He is said to have read his own translation of Horace's "Diffugere nives" ("The snows are fled away"—Horace, *Odes* iv. 7; later published by Laurence Housman as *More Poems*, poem V) in the course of a lecture in 1914; according to one account, at the end of his lecture Housman read his translation of "Diffugere nives" and then spoke: "'That,' he said hurriedly, almost like a man betraying a secret, 'I regard as the most beautiful poem in ancient literature' and walked quickly out of the room."[8]

Horace's odes had of course been an important part of the traditional education in the classics in England (among those portions of the English population who were allowed classical education). Horace was, for example, one of the poets on whom Housman was required to write an essay for his scholarship examination at St. John's College, Oxford, in 1877. The importance of Horace's odes in the formation of Housman's poetry can be quickly illustrated, as in the following passage (from C. E. Bennett's prose translation of Horace's Latin verse): "Now is the fitting time to garland our glistening locks with myrtle green or with the blossoms that the unfettered earth brings forth . . . Pale Death with foot impartial knocks at the poor man's cottage and at princes' palaces. . . . life's brief span forbids thy entering on far-reaching hopes."[9] The analogy with Housman's poem is obvious—especially the call to momentary flowerings of beauty against a backdrop of inevitable death and nothingness. In English poetry of the 1890s, that theme and even the interest in that specific example from Horace was in fact widespread: in 1896, for example, the same year in which *A Shropshire Lad* was published, Ernest Dowson published a volume entitled *Verses* and including one of his best-known lyrics, which takes for its title the last line from that passage I have just quoted from Horace—*vitae summa brevis spem nos incohare longam* ("life's brief span forbids thy entering on far-reaching hopes").[10]

The affinity of Housman's atheism with pagan thought and feeling, especially the Epicurean (or Cyrenaic) theme of enhancing pleasure or happiness during a brief human life, is often very clear and effective, as in *A Shropshire Lad*, poem LVII: "I shall have lived a little while / Before I die for ever." Like ice and fire, delight and pain or beauty and bitterness are juxtaposed (by Housman and coincidentally in the same year by Dowson) in the little fictions that the poems present. Where their song-like loveliness and ease might have led to sentimentality, the central theme of the book—the pathos and integrity of its honest recognition of the finality of death—prevents any such illusion:

> Bring baskets now, and sally
> Upon the spring's array,
> And bear from hill and valley
> The daffodil away
> That dies on Easter day. (XXIX, "The Lent Lily")

Housman, Dowson, and in fact all educated poets of the period recognized that these Epicurean themes are not unique to the Greek Anthology and Horace, or to classical poetry, but appear widely elsewhere, too, including the Bible. In a letter to Laurence Housman, Housman writes of their sister Katharine's response to his book of poems: "Kate writes to say that she likes the verse better than the sentiments. The sentiments, she then goes on to say, appear to be taken from the book of Ecclesiastes. To prefer my versification to the sentiments of the Holy Ghost is decidedly flattering, but strikes me as a trifle impious" (*Letters*, 37). Though Housman writes here with a sense of humor, his sister has correctly identified some shared moral and emotional content. The following passage from Ecclesiastes, for example, expresses the "sentiments" to which Katharine Housman refers, including skepticism about supposed immortality and a resulting Epicurean or Cyrenaic ethics:

> that which befalleth the sons of men befalleth beasts; even one thing befalleth them: as the one dieth, so dieth the other; yea, they have all one breath; so that a man hath no preeminence above a beast: for all is vanity.
>
> All go unto one place; all are of the dust, and all turn to dust again.
>
> Who knoweth the spirit of man that goeth upward, and the spirit of the beast that goeth downward to the earth?
>
> Wherefore I perceive that a man should rejoice in his own works; for that is his portion: for who shall bring him to see what shall be after him?
>
> (Ecclesiastes 3: 19–22; Authorized Version)

The similarity to lyrics from the Greek Anthology is striking, as for example this translation from Asklepiades's "To His Mistress": "There are no lovers, dear, in the under world, / No love but here"; "below . . . dust and ashes / Will be our only lying down together."[11] And the similarity to Housman's poetry is again striking:

> Lovers lying two and two
> Ask not whom they sleep beside,
> And the bridegroom all night through
> Never turns him to the bride. (*A Shropshire Lad*, XII)

Clearly, Housman's poetry needs to be understood within these contexts—the literary context of ancient, biblical, and contemporary poetry, and the historical context of Victorian England. As T. S. Eliot writes, "No poet, no artist of any art, has his complete meaning alone."[12] The poems are not autobiographical expressions of his own personal feelings. As Housman said very plainly, "the Shropshire Lad is an imaginary figure. . . . Very little in the book is biographical" (*Letters*, 328). In a letter to his brother Laurence, Housman indicates (again humorously) how false is the impression that the poems in *A Shropshire Lad* are expressions of his personal experience. After the book had appeared, Housman discovered that Hughley Church could not, in fact, "have much of a steeple," in contrast to what he had written in his poem, "Hughley Steeple" (*A Shropshire Lad*, LXI). He had written without knowing whether the church had a steeple or not (*Letters*, 39). The poem mentions that suicides are buried at the north side of the church. Laurence Housman writes that Housman walked to Hughley to see the church and its steeple (after Housman's poem had appeared in print); "when I reached it, I found that the 'far-known sign' was buried away in a valley," and instead of "suicides" they were mostly "churchwardens and wives of Vicars" who are buried at the north side of the church. Housman reportedly told Laurence that he used the name "Hughley Steeple" because of its sound (Laurence's report of that statement appears in Symons, 36). And Housman mentions that Matthew Arnold had been likewise inaccurate about local detail in Arnold's poem "The Church at Brou."

Housman's poems are about other and larger things than Hughley, or steeples, or Shropshire, or particular lads, or Housman's personal experiences. In the same letter (5 October 1896) Housman writes, "Morris dead!" (*Letters*, 39), referring to the news of the death of the great poet, artist, and socialist, and anticipating that Swinburne would write a poem about Morris's death. It is clear that Housman was no socialist; in fact he sometimes expressed doubts about the wisdom even of democracy, perhaps frivolously or perhaps in accord with a statement made by the central character in Arnold's *Empedocles on Etna*, where Empedocles says that a great multitude of small-minded people can become a powerful force but not a wise one (see act 2, lines 93–94). What his interest in contemporary writers (including Swinburne and Morris) expresses is not an agreement on political issues, but rather a larger matter: the transposition into poetry, frequently with classical allusions, of the politically dangerous but intellectually compelling changes brought about by modern science and history.

An outstanding example, and apparently Housman's favorite, is *Empedocles on Etna*, which Pollard said Housman recommended "as containing 'all the law and the prophets'" (See Pollard's essay in Symons, 31). (The biblical allusion is obviously ironic; Housman uses the phrase to mean simply necessary wisdom.) There Arnold uses the ancient philosopher as a vehicle for voicing tendencies in specifically modern thought. For example, Empedocles voices the realization that religion is a fantasy and a projection that people make up because they prefer comforting illusions to hard (naturalistic) truths (see act 1, lines 277–80, 304–305, 347–50, 402–406). And the ancient atomistic theory is a vehicle that Arnold uses in *Empedocles on Etna* as Housman uses it in *A Shropshire Lad* XXXI, XXXII, and XXXVIII: like everything else in the world, a person is made of matter and energy, "the stuff of life," which is formed into new objects (or animals) in a natural cycle of decay and organic formation.

Like the factual implications, the *ethical* implications that follow from modern naturalism (as likewise from ancient atomism) are also widespread concerns in the Victorian period, as in the Epicureanism of Housman and many others, though this way of thought frequently required suppression or softening for public consumption. To cite one highly influential example, the Epicureanism of Walter Pater is probably most widely known with reference to the following passage from the conclusion to his book, *The Renaissance*: "we have an interval, and then our place knows us no more. Some spend this interval in listlessness, some in high passions, the wisest . . . in art and song. For our one chance lies in expanding that interval, in getting as many pulsations as possible into the given time. Great passions may give us this quickened sense of life, ecstasy and sorrow of love. . . . Of such wisdom, the poetic passion, the desire of beauty, the love of art for its own sake, has most."[13] In the first edition of *The Renaissance*, Pater had used the phrase "political or religious enthusiasms" negatively, but in an age in which traditional Christian orthodoxy was still wielding power in England, he suppressed the conclusion entirely from the second edition of the book, and in the third he deleted the reference to "political or religious enthusiasms," which (like the Epicurean content of the essay at large) was likely to have offended the orthodox and the powerful. Housman had read Pater—including the novel *Marius the Epicurean*, which develops the thoughts of this essay more fully (see *Letters*, 424)—but he was understandably cautious and guarded when he publicly expressed his admiration (see *Prose*, 198).

Besides Arnold and Swinburne, poets whom Housman admired include Shakespeare and William Blake (both of whose lyrics Housman praises in "The Name and Nature of Poetry"), Thomas Hardy (see *Letters*, 329), and Edna St. Vincent Millay, whom he called "the best living American poet" (*Letters*, 315). Laurence Housman records that "another of Alfred's high admirations was Christina Rossetti, of whom he said that posterity would probably place her above Swinburne" (L. Housman, 86). Of the influence of classical poetry on his own poems, Housman wrote that "no doubt I have been unconsciously influenced by the Greeks and Latins, but I was surprised when critics spoke of my poetry as 'classical.' Its chief sources of which I am conscious are Shakespeare's songs, the Scottish border ballads and Heine" (*Letters*, 329). The relationship between Housman's poetry and the great poem of Lucretius, *De rerum natura (The Nature of the Universe)*, has been discussed helpfully by Haber (Haber 1967, 155–65), and the relationship of Housman's thought to classical skepticism has been the subject of studies by Terence Allan Hoagwood.[14]

The interest and excellence of Housman's poems, however, lie not in their moral or philosophical content, which, as I have tried to suggest, is rather traditional; the poems' outstanding features are matters of artistry. For example, "Loveliest of Trees" (*A Shropshire Lad* II) achieves an intensity of feeling in its last line ("To see the cherry hung with snow") that has helped to make it one of the most widely read and admired lyrics in all of English literature, despite the simplicity of its language, and despite the fact that the line is made of only eight syllables. Part of its effect derives from the use of *snow* to designate the white petals of the flowering cherry tree: snow is, of course, a cold image whose associations in poetry are often morbid. In context, the poem's speaker is resolving to seek beauty and joy, though they are fleeting; because the speaker has been reflecting on death, this turn to beauty is made poignant and complex by the subtle effect of chilling that *snow* brings into the line. Further, the meter, about which Housman was meticulous, is perfect: whereas three earlier lines had used carefully placed variants in the meter, the perfectly regular iambic rhythm here adds a stately sound to the line, making a fit music for the statement of the speaker's firm resolve. This firmness is counterpointed by the fragility of the white petals of the flower (and the blossoms of cherry trees are, in fact, quite beautiful but also short-lived). Like the contrast between joy in the spring and snow, this contrast between firmness and fragility produces a complexity of feeling that is remarkable given the simple (and few) words that Housman has used.

These effects, whose explanation can sound so plotted, are not necessarily the result of conscious intentions, as for example the features of a work of mechanical drawing would be the result of conscious intentions. Instead, as Housman later stated very clearly in "The Name and Nature of Poetry," artistic intensity emerges from deeper, unconscious levels of feeling and from keen sensitivity to the language and its music, and not from rational intelligence or self-conscious "meaning." In fact, self-conscious intention sometimes needs to be overcome; for example, in the unique draft of the poem, Housman had written explicitly of an emotion in the first line of the final stanza: "And since to look on things you love."[15] That phrase was replaced, however, with a line that presents loveliness in physical imagery, rather than baldly reporting an emotion explicitly: "And since to look at things in bloom." The poem's speaker has been counting the years that remain before his death, and the relevant feeling here, as he voices a determination to see beauty while he can, could hardly be more clear. Self-consciousness *about* having a feeling is very different from *creating* that feeling in music and imagery, and it is this creation of artistic feeling that Housman has achieved.

For that reason, narrowly biographical interpretation of poems is misleading. For example, the death of Housman's father about six months before Housman wrote the poem may have awakened painful feelings about the brevity of a human life and may have intensified Housman's feeling that beauty and delight must be seized quickly before the inevitable nothingness of death. But to focus on Housman's father here, in response to the poem, would distract one from the poem's artistry, which is a matter of language and not family experience. Another death—of Adalbert Jackson, for example, who died in 1892, or the death of one's own relative, or friend, or anybody else—could serve as an example as fitly as the death of Edward Housman; the idea (*carpe diem*) and the feeling are poetic and not biographical; the poem is special for its artistry rather than its "meaning," in the ordinary sense.

Factual and historical information is important for interpreting the poem, but not because biographical translations are helpful—they are not. The removal of traditional and comforting illusions about an afterlife (whether in Elysian fields or "heaven") was a central tendency of the nineteenth century, involving science as well as philosophy and the arts, as I have previously suggested. For Lucretius (who attacked superstition in the first century B.C.) and for Victorians (whose more scientific understanding of a similarly naturalistic worldview is expressed by Huxley), the discrediting of fairy tales about an imaginary afterlife involved discoveries about the composition and decomposition of matter, including organic matter. For Housman and for educated Victorians generally, the importance of human life and its joys was intensified by recognition that every individual life is fragile and temporary.

Housman's personal knowledge of the relationship between ancient pagan materialism and modern science is evident: for example, in a letter of 11 June 1900, he writes about eugenics, a new science (first named *eugenics* in Francis Galton's *Inquiries into Human Faculty and Development* [1883]) that extended the theory of evolution and knowledge of genetics into the development of improved breeding of species—and specifically human beings. The first Professor of Eugenics was Karl Pearson (at the University of London), and Housman writes to his friend Lily Thicknesse, "On Saturday Karl Pearson and I are going for a walk in Buckinghamshire, to find a farmer who lays a particular kind of eggs, which tend to prove that there is no God" (*Letters*, 52–53). Housman's writing in that humorous tone suggests both his familiarity with the conflicts surrounding the science and his own ironic and critical perspective on the matter.

Further, the many poems in *A Shropshire Lad* about war, and particularly war in distant lands, take on more specific meanings when they are interpreted in terms of the historical context in which Housman wrote them. In Housman's lifetime, Nigeria, East Africa, and Rhodesia came under British commercial domination and then British governmental rule. In 1876, Queen Victoria was declared Empress of India. Burma and Malaysia were annexed to the empire. Egypt and the Sudan came under British rule. The Suez Canal was opened in 1870, and it was of great importance for the British Empire, facilitating commerce with India. In 1882, Britain invaded Egypt (and Britain continued to occupy that country until 1954). British military campaigns in the 1880s and 1890s resulted in the annexing of the Sudan. The Cape of Good Hope had been occupied in 1795 to protect the British trade route to India; in 1877, a government of confederation was imposed by the British upon the resident Boers (Dutch people in southern Africa); in 1879, the British exterminated the Zulus. In 1880–81, the first Boer War was fought, and the second Boer War, in which Housman's brother Herbert died, was fought 1899–1902.[16] When Housman writes (as often in his poetry he does) of the futility, deadliness, and senseless disaster of war, he is not simply recording eternal truths in an abstract or emotional way, but responding to pressing and important realities.

Besides his own poetry, and besides the classical scholarship which was always his main professional work, Housman also helped his brother Laurence to write and rewrite poems, commenting in detail, for example, on the manuscript of Laurence's first collection of poems, *Green Arras*. Housman's advice is constructive in that it is almost wholly negative, pointing out changes that need to be made in the poems; his most general advice is that the poems are obscure because Laurence has failed to take into account a reader's point of view (*Letters*, 31–34). The brothers' shared interests also appear when Housman responds to Laurence's novel, *Gods and Their Makers*: Housman refers to his brother, good-naturedly in the manner of a shared joke, as "thou irreligious writer" (*Letters*, 41–42).

In September 1897, Housman writes to his stepmother of a month's vacation in Europe which he has just completed. He visited Paris, Rome, and Naples, and he writes of Notre Dame and other churches, of the Louvre, Pompeii, Vesuvius (its ashes and sulphur), and also the objects of beauty—flowers, for example, and museums—that interested him especially. Housman subsequently took trips to Europe almost every year. Graves suggests that Paris was a favorite resort for Housman in part because "it offered a rich diet of sexual adventures" (Graves 1979, 155); Page denies that Housman's trips to Paris "were no more than sexual escapades," pointing out, for example, that Housman's frequent visits to cathedral towns expressed other interests (Page, 121). While this question has been treated as a controversy, clearly Graves does not say that the trips were *only* sexual escapades, and both Graves and Page are sensitive to the fact that Housman was interested in larger and more important issues than merely personal behavior.

When Housman does evidently write about homosexuality, it is not a personal indulgence or problem, but a social and moral issue of large importance to which he devotes the poem: for example, one of the poems by Housman that his brother Laurence published after his death is widely understood to refer to the trial and imprisonment of Oscar Wilde, on charges of indecent (i.e., homosexual) conduct. Even if the poem used homosexuality as an example of customary societal brutality and intolerance, and even if Wilde's case were the poem's central example, the poem is about cruelty—not personal, but societal cruelty—and it is about intolerance, ignorance, and injustice, and the suffering that these things bring upon innocent people. The poem says that a young man is being taken "to prison for the colour of his hair"—that is, he is being punished by society for the way that he was made, without his will. Bigotry is satirized:

> 'Tis a shame to human nature, such a head of hair as his;
> In the good old time 'twas hanging for the colour that it is;
> Though hanging isn't bad enough and flaying would be fair
> For the nameless and abominable colour of his hair. (233)

In a poem that Housman did publish, homosexuality may or may not have been in the poet's mind, and may or may not be a relevant example, but the larger issues—moral freedom, widespread bigotry, intolerance, and cruelty—are more clear and more important than any merely personal inclinations of the poet, or of Wilde, or of any other individual:

> let God and man decree
> Laws for themselves and not for me;
>
> .   .   .   .
> . . . they
> Need only look the other way.
> But no, they will not; they must still
> Wrest their neighbour to their will,
> And make me dance as they desire
> With jail and gallows and hell-fire. (*Last Poems*, XII)

In 1899, Housman met Thomas Hardy, who had been (according to A. W. Pollard) Housman's favorite novelist (Symons, 31). Housman later visited Hardy at his home in Dorchester, contributed a poem to a volume to be dedicated to Hardy, dined with him at Cambridge, and served as a pallbearer at Hardy's funeral. Pollard writes that he thought Hardy's influence on Housman was more profound, even, than the influence of Arnold. Some of Hardy's poems are comparable with some of Housman's, including their antiwar poems (such as Hardy's "Drummer Hodge" and "A Wife in London") and their poems repudiating the comforting illusions of idealism; often in works by both Hardy and Housman characters voice unwittingly a vain and tragically hollow optimism within the frame of a naturalistic world, without providence or divine meaning, in which they are inevitably destroyed (see, for example, Hardy's "Hap" and "The Subalterns").

In 1901, Housman's brother Herbert died in the Boer War, having enlisted in the King's Royal Rifles 11 years earlier, and having served in India and in Burma before going to fight in southern Africa. Though the British had seized control of the larger Boer cities in 1900, the Boers continued fighting. H. C. G. Matthew summarizes: "The British replied by burning Boer farms, clearing the veldt, and systematically herding Boer families into 'concentration camps.' High death rates in the camps led to radical protests in Britain" (p. 565). The war ended (with a negotiated settlement rather than a total defeat of the Boers) in 1902. In the meanwhile, Herbert Housman had died while participating in a charge of mounted infantry, attempting to regain some guns from the Boers (Symons, 26).

Housman's life surely included its pleasures, however, as well as its sorrows. For example, his nearly annual vacations to the Continent evidently remained an important part of his routine. From 1900 to 1908, his trips included stays in Venice, where he admired the Cathedral of St. Mark, "the most beautiful, not the grandest, building in the world" (*Letters*, 57). He also examined, and described in his letters, other buildings—chiefly churches and palaces—making architectural observations. He also studied paintings in Venice, admiring most those of Giovanni Bellini and liking less those of Tintoretto and Paolo Veronese (*Letters*, 58). He describes the wildflowers to be found near Venice and the butterflies. He also mentions his meeting a gondolier "who has had one eye kicked out by a horse" (*Letters*, 58). (Graves has said, and Page has doubted, that Housman had a love affair with this gondolier, whose name was Andrea [see Graves 1979, 151–53; Page, 122–23].)

In 1903, Housman published the first volume of his edition and commentary on Manilius's *Astronomica*, which he intended to be his major work in classical studies. (He published the second book in 1912, the third in 1916, the fourth in 1920, and the fifth in 1930.) He did not think that Manilius's poem was the most admirable among ancient Latin poems, but he found that scholarly problems made it the most interesting and promising for his work. Available editions needed correcting. His preface to the first volume (reprinted in *Prose*, 23–44) articulates some principles of textual criticism that have remained permanently important in classical studies. Housman's arguments involve the conflict between scholars who follow one surviving manuscript of a given ancient

work, wherever possible, and those who instead argue for the importance of vigorous and methodical comparison of all available manuscripts
and editions, with careful analysis of linguistic detail, to construct upon
the best evidence a new, critical text, rather than reproduce an existing
text as closely as possible. Housman was harshly critical of scholars who
relied on one authoritative source.

Another scholarly issue to which Housman contributes an important
principle concerns the method of choosing between alternative versions
of a passage when manuscript sources disagree. Housman argues that it
is unwise to assume in every instance that the version that makes most
apparent sense is the correct one. He suggests that scribes, copyists, and
editors are more likely to alter a difficult text by making it easier than by
making it more difficult; in consequence, the correct version of a passage
on which manuscripts disagree may be the one that makes least apparent sense. Housman argues that the task of a textual critic cannot be
simplified by a general rule (such as the following of one manuscript
source consistently); a textual critic must make an informed and critical
decision in each case. His five volumes of Manilius's *Astronomica* include
hundreds of pages of very specific argument, in Latin, in very fine print,
about minute scholarly details.

Housman's own essays, however—even when he is making scholarly
arguments as in the prefaces to his volumes of Manilius—are never dull;
his prose is an example of art. T. S. Eliot wrote in 1933 that Housman
"is one of the few living masters of English prose" and that, on
Housman's chosen subjects, "there is no one living who can write better"; and Eliot mentions the preface of Manilius. Eliot identifies the
excellence of Housman's prose as "a certain emotional intensity"—not,
he says, "explicit emotion" or feelings that Housman mentions, but
rather "the intensity of the artist . . . capable of informing any subject
matter."[17] To quote statements pertaining to the two issues of scholarly
method that I have mentioned will briefly illustrate Housman's style: on
the procedure of following one manuscript consistently, he writes, "An
editor of no judgment, perpetually confronted with a couple of MSS. to
choose from, cannot but feel in every fibre of his being that he is a don-
key between two bundles of hay. What shall he do now? Leave criticism
to critics, you may say, and betake himself to any honest trade for which
he is less unfit. But he prefers a more flattering solution: he confusedly
imagines that if one bundle of hay is removed he will cease to be a don-
key" (*Prose*, 35). Housman connects this issue, the consistent preference

of one manuscript, with the second issue, having to do with the likelihood of an author's having actually written the version that makes least
apparent sense:

> Suppose, if you will, that the editor's "best MS." is in truth the best; his
> way of using it is none the less ridiculous. To believe that wherever a best
> MS. gives possible readings it gives true readings, and that only where it
> gives impossible readings does it give false readings, is to believe that an
> incompetent editor is the darling of Providence, which has given its
> angels charge over him lest at any time his sloth and folly should produce
> their natural results and incur their appropriate penalty. (*Prose*, 36)

Housman does not only exhibit wit (as in that ridicule of "an incompe-
tent editor"), but his prose sometimes rises eloquently to large and
important issues, having to do with his view of life and not only with
scholarly details. The following passage makes humorous comparison of
the importance of narrow, scholarly details with greater human problems, but it also culminates in an important and beautifully written
statement of an ethical skepticism that appears often in Housman's
poetry and prose alike: "Chance and the common course of nature will
not bring it to pass that the readings of a MS. are right wherever they
are possible and impossible wherever they are wrong: that needs divine
intervention; and when one considers the history of man and the specta-
cle of the universe I hope one may say without impiety that divine intervention might have been better employed elsewhere. How the world is
managed, and why it was created, I cannot tell; but it is no feather-bed
for the repose of sluggards" (*Prose*, 36).

Chapter Three
Kennedy Professor of Latin, Cambridge

Since 1889 (three years before he became Professor of Latin at University College), Housman had been a member of the Cambridge Philological Society, to which he had been invited on the basis of his scholarly publications. There he maintained friendships with other classical scholars, including Henry Jackson, who had been the editor of the *Journal of Philology* when Housman began publishing classical papers there. In 1911, Housman was appointed Kennedy Professor of Latin at the University of Cambridge, and Fellow of Trinity College, Cambridge, and he remained in those positions for the rest of his life. On 9 May 1911, he delivered a lecture at Cambridge, the Inaugural Lecture. Housman never allowed publication of this lecture, because he was unable to verify a scholarly point mentioned in the lecture, concerning the text of a poem by Shelley, but it was published long after his death (first in a nearly complete version in the *Times Literary Supplement*, 9 May 1968, and then, with the title, *The Confines of Criticism*, in 1969).[1] Here, Housman explains that classical scholarship is not literary criticism; for Housman, scholarship is not concerned with aesthetic appreciation of poetry, but rather factual knowledge: "Scholarship, that study of the ancient literatures for which chairs of Greek and Latin are founded, is itself a department . . . not of literature but of science; and science ought to be scientific and ought not to be literary" (*Confines*, 26).

In the course of explaining the differences between scholarly work and aesthetic appreciation, however, Housman writes of other issues, including the power of prejudice: "It is unfortunately true that audiences in general are fond of being told what they know already, and that the desire of most readers and hearers is not to be given thoughts which are new and true, but thoughts which, whether true or false, are their own thoughts, and which they rejoice to recognize dressed up in the current variety of academic journalese, and tricked out with an assortment of popular adjectives" (*Confines*, 27–28). He writes of historical relativity, too, producing an example that illustrates one of his central principles of scholarly work:

> When Horace is reported to have said *seu mobilibus ueris inhorruit adventus foliis*, and when pedants like Bentley and Munro object that the phrase is unsuitable to its context, of what avail is it to be assured by persons of taste—that is to say persons of British taste, Victorian taste, and sub-Tennysonian taste—that these are exquisite lines? Exquisite to whom? Consider the mutations of opinion, the reversals of literary judgment, which this one small island has witnessed in the last 150 years: what is the likelihood that your notions or your contemporaries' notions of the exquisite are those of a foreigner who wrote for foreigners two millenniums ago? And for what foreigners? For the Romans, for men whose religion you disbelieve, whose chief institution you abominate, whose manners you do not like to talk about, but whose literary tastes, you flatter yourself, were identical with yours. No: in this aspect we must learn to say of our tastes what Isaiah says of our righteousness: they are as filthy rags. (*Confines*, 34)

Appreciations of poetry had already, in Housman's lifetime, included the pitch for personal identification, pretending that a poet in a different century expressed one's own personal feelings, rather than different feelings pertinent to the poet's different life and time. Likewise popular was the illusion of eternal truth, which is an escapist's denial that earthly history changes everything, including people's ideas and tastes. Housman acknowledges that people like those illusions, but he indicates that they *are* illusions, and that scholarship should reckon with the facts of historical difference rather than the pleasing falsehoods of sentimental enjoyment.

While he continued to view his professional life as that of a scholar, and not a poet, his own poetry became increasingly popular. In 1915, Housman granted permission for the printing of some of his poems in a collection of poetry to be supplied to soldiers in World War I, "in one of the *Times Broadsheets* for the trenches" (*Letters*, 140). Apparently the idea was that patriotic poetry would be comforting or inspirational for soldiers, and somehow the compiler (Walter Raleigh) evidently thought that Housman's poetry was patriotic. This opinion about Housman's poetry is astonishing, because the poems about war in *A Shropshire Lad* are satirically critical of the war, and furthermore there is evidence that Housman was personally hostile to the war and to warriors. In 1914 he characterized the patriotism of soldiers in this way: "the thirst for blood is raging among the youth of England" (*Letters*, 136). When buildings at Cambridge were used as temporary housing for soldiers, he complained in a letter that "here we have 1000 undergraduates and 20,000 soldiers, 500 of them billeted in the building in which I write" (*Letters*, 138). He ridicules the war and military preparations: "I have three nephews being inoculated for typhoid and catching pneumonia on Salisbury Plain and performing other acts of war calculated to make the German Emperor realise that he is a very misguided man" (*Letters*, 136). Page writes that there is no evidence that Housman ever spoke to any of the soldiers housed at Cambridge, and he reproduces a couplet that Housman wrote, ridiculing the soldiers' smoking cheap cigarettes and indulging in sexual excesses (Page, 112).

In view of these facts, it is also astonishing that Laurence Housman writes of Housman that "at the beginning of the War [World War I] he sent the Chancellor a donation of several hundred pounds" (L. Housman, 1938, 110). Laurence Housman mentions throughout his biography of Housman (as others generally do not) that Housman was interested in national and international politics, and his statement that Housman donated money to the National Government in 1931 (when poverty, unemployment, hunger marches, and demonstrations in violently depressed regions were worsening during the Great Depression) is less puzzling; but the statement by his brother that the antiwar poet sent money to support the war remains a riddle. Housman's reticence or secrecy about his politics (as likewise about many other matters) makes the riddle a difficult one to solve. As his friend Percy Withers wrote, shortly after Housman's death, "the depths and complexities of Housman's character were almost impenetrably obscured by his reticence, and still more perhaps by his determined habit of self-suppression."[2] Laurence Housman says simply, "in politics he stayed aloof" (L. Housman 1938, 106).

Reasons for Housman's not publicizing his negative attitudes about the war are obvious: Bertrand Russell was a friend of Housman's at Cambridge in these years, and when Russell was convicted in 1916 for his antiwar activities he was also removed from his position as lecturer at Cambridge. After the war, several Fellows at Cambridge signed a letter petitioning for Russell's reinstatement, and Housman wrote that he had agreed with Russell in opposing military conscription "at the time, though I now see I was wrong."[3] Again, this evidence makes it odd that Housman was said to have donated "several hundred pounds" to support a war effort that by his own admission he opposed.

Another problem worsened during the war years: censorship. Not only publications, but also mail was censored. Housman wrote to Edmund Gosse, whose letters had been intercepted by the censor, criticizing the practice and ridiculing the stupidity of persons working in the censor's office (*Letters*, 137). Housman's "buried life" had of course *been* buried since his youth, and it remained so; the censorship of the mail is not a cause of Housman's secrecy, but another example of the circumstances that led him to it.

In October 1922, Housman's second book of poems, *Last Poems*, appeared; it was the last book of poems he ever published. Though some of the poems were new—several were not written until 1922, according to dates supplied by Housman—some were not (several date from 1895).[4] Some were written at the time of the Boer War in which his brother Herbert had died—including "Lancer":

> I 'listed at home for a lancer,
> *Oh who would not sleep with the brave?*
> I 'listed at home for a lancer
> To ride on a horse to my grave. (p. 103)

One of the poems in *Last Poems*, "Illic Jacet," had first been published in a periodical (*The Academy*) in 1900, and it, too, notices the irony that many of the slain had volunteered for this: looking at the grave of a freshly buried soldier, the poem's speaker says,

> Oh dark is the chamber and lonely,
> And lights and companions depart;
> But lief will he lose them and only
> Behold the desire of his heart. (p. 101)

When he learned that the third son of Housman's sister Katharine was killed in World War I (in 1915), Housman sent her a copy of "Illic Jacet," with a letter indicating that "I remember your telling me at the beginning of the war that he had almost a hope and expectation of dying in battle" (*Letters*, 141).

The poems in *Last Poems* are not, however, limited in their reference to particular wars, or even to war in general, but use the example of war to raise larger issues: a soldier considers his military destination and says "Too fast to yonder strand forlorn / We journey" (p. 98); obviously "we" are human beings (and not merely these soldiers) and the distant strand to which "we" journey too fast is not merely this or that war, this or that battlefield death, but death itself. In "Grenadier," a soldier who was recruited with a promise of "thirteen pence a day" is wounded and dying, and this example leads the soldier to a reflection that (again like Ecclesiastes) denies immortality and laments the total nothingness that follows a brief human life: "For in the grave, they say, / Is neither knowledge nor device / Nor thirteen pence a day" (p. 102). Even more explicit is poem IX, "The chestnut casts his flambeaux":

> It is in truth iniquity on high
> To cheat our sentenced souls of aught they crave,
> And mar the merriment as you and I
> Fare on our long fool's-errand to the grave.
>
> .   .   .   .
>
> Our only portion is the estate of man:
> We want the moon, but we shall get no more.
>
> .   .   .   .
>
> The flesh will grieve on other bones than ours
> Soon, and the soul will mourn in other breasts.
> The troubles of our proud and angry dust
> Are from eternity, and shall not fail.

The poem (like the book as a whole) does not rest in that voice of pessimism, but comically the poem portrays the speaker—not an admirable character at all—clamoring for ale ("pass the can") and (juxtaposing the sublime and the ridiculous) advising a comrade, "Shoulder the sky, my lad, and drink your ale" (p. 108).

Housman's life, like his poetry, was neither humorless nor gloomy, though those who could perceive only the obvious surface (of his poetry or his life) might have been deceived. Laurence Housman quotes a letter from Housman's sister-in-law: "There is one thing I don't understand in all that is written about Alfred—they all speak as if he never had any happiness in life; surely that cannot be true. I never knew that side of his life, he always seemed to enjoy things and to be happy, and enjoy amusing others with his clever nonsense. I have known him and Basil [Housman's brother] laugh until they cried" (L. Housman 1938, 96). Laurence Housman writes that "he kept himself rigidly aloof from all but a small circle of friends," and that whereas "some found him impenetrably silent, others [found him] genially conversational." Laurence writes that, after Housman had visited Robert Bridges (who was appointed Poet Laureate in 1913), he "wrote telling me how very well they had agreed on certain important literary and political matters" (L. Housman 1938, 94–95).

Housman's friends and acquaintances included such important figures in the intellectual history of England (and the world) that one hopes that Housman's putative reticence did not inhibit conversation: he knew and admired Russell, as I have said, and he knew Ludwig Wittgenstein (a neighbor of Housman at Cambridge). Housman knew Sir James George Frazer, whose book *The Golden Bough* is among the more influential books of social anthropology ever written; Housman was chosen to compose a celebratory address to Frazer on the occasion of the founding of a lectureship in his name (*Letters*, 184), and Housman contributed information about a fire festival in Capri (based on his own visit) that Frazer used in the *Golden Bough* (Page, 77).

In 1918, Housman met André Gide, a French writer whose novels, plays, poems, and essays include (like some of Housman's writings) celebrations of a life of pleasure, with questioning of moral codes and their value, and who (in the dialogues entitled *Corydon*) defended homosexuality. Housman wrote in a letter to another friend that he had met Gide and hoped to see him again (*Letters*, 156).

Housman's naturalism always involved the ethical implications of Epicurean or Cyrenaic thinking, but it also involved the understanding of the natural and material world *as* natural and material, leading him to prefer science over religion or myth as a means of seeking truth. His friends and acquaintances at Cambridge included some of the foremost scientists of the twentieth century: Joseph John Thompson, for example, who discovered the existence of electrons (for which he received the Nobel Prize in 1906), and Ernest Rutherford, whose work with radioactivity and atomic fragments brought him the Nobel Prize in 1908, and who first proposed the (currently accepted) model of the atom, consisting of a positively charged nucleus and negatively charged electrons at a distance from the nucleus.

Housman corresponded with T. S. Eliot, replying in 1926 to an invitation from Eliot to write an introduction to a book by Wilkie Collins.

He also corresponded with Bridges, who sent him a copy of the poems of Gerard Manley Hopkins, and Housman's letter of thanks includes his careful assessment of Hopkins's poetry (*Letters*, 158–59). In addition to his admiration for the work of his friend Hardy and for the poetry of Arnold, Housman expressed his response to the work of numerous English poets, though many of his papers were destroyed (by his order) to prevent their publication; for example, a fragment of a paper on Arnold is all that survives of his lectures given to the University College Literary Society (*Prose*, 196–98).

In the autobiographical summary that he sent to Pollet in 1933, Housman mentioned Heinrich Heine among the "chief sources" of his poetry: Heine (1797–1856) was a German writer whose poetry includes lyrics of extraordinary beauty in sound, imagery, and feeling, often involving dreams, erotic love, and enchantment; Heine's poems, however, frequently turn from moments of apparent or illusory loveliness to end in bitterness, sorrow, disillusionment, and death. A German-born Jew living as if in exile in Paris for much of his professional life, Heine also wrote critically and effectively about politics, history, society, and ideology.

Housman wrote short pieces on some English poets, including Shelley (*Times Literary Supplement*, 20 December 1928; see *Letters*, 271–72) and Keats (*Times Literary Supplement*, 8 May 1924; *Letters*, 219–20), but these are very limited in their reference, having to do with particular words in particular lines of the poets' work. Far more generally, and far more memorably, his thoughts on poetry and poets are expressed in the essay that, more than any other, deserves comparison with the literary essays of Matthew Arnold and T. S. Eliot: "The Name and Nature of Poetry," Housman's last great and influential work, which was delivered as the Leslie Stephen Lecture at Cambridge on 9 May 1933.

Here, Housman indicates that the special function of poetry is not "to transmit thought" but rather "to transfuse emotion" (*Prose*, 172). Housman's survey of the kinds of poetry that flourished in the eighteenth century agrees with Arnold's earlier observation that the faculty of rational, conscious, and therefore relatively superficial thought had flourished in that period, producing valuable prose and carefully written verse but not often great poetry in a more profound sense of that word; "Man had ceased to live from the depths of his nature" (*Prose*, 176). Like other modern thinkers, including saliently T. S. Eliot, Housman argues that poetry emerges from, and speaks to, those unconscious depths rather than the merely rational mind whose needs are best served by prose.

The theme of the unconscious is one of the modernist features of Housman's argument in "The Name and Nature of Poetry," and another modernist feature concerns his representation of poetry as an operation of language as opposed to a conveyance of ideas. For example, Housman writes that the conventions of "poetic diction" (a conventional and even explicitly approved vocabulary for poems) worsened matters for the poetry of the eighteenth century; "this deadening of language . . . worked inward, and deadened perception" (p. 178). Comparably with T. S. Eliot, Housman suggests that what is most important in poetry is not its meaning, not its explicit content (moral or otherwise), but the artistic intensity with which it generates profound feeling; he suggests that people who enjoy religious poetry, for example, are probably not enjoying the poetry in it at all, but rather something else "which they like better than poetry" (*Prose*, 185). "Opinions and beliefs," he says, "are distinct from poetry itself" (*Prose*, 186); poetry is not a feature of ideas that can be communicated, but rather an artistry in "the words in which the idea is clothed" (*Prose*, 187). The most poetical of poets (Housman mentions Shakespeare and Blake) produce poems "adulterated with so little meaning that nothing except poetical emotion is perceived and matters" (*Prose*, 189); and this poetical emotion arises from (and speaks to) "some region deeper than the mind" (*Prose*, 192).

In his last years, Housman was sometimes troubled with worsening health, but he retained his active sense of humor. For example, less than a year before his death he wrote to Laurence Housman about climbing the steps to the rooms in which he lived at Trinity College, Cambridge: "I still go up my 44 stairs two at a time, but that is in hopes of dropping dead at the top" (*Letters*, 370). (Housman had written humorously about suicide long before. For example, in 1913 he wrote to Alice Rothenstein about the disagreeable chore of grading examination papers at Cambridge: "if you ever have to examine for University Scholarships you will find as I do that all one's leisure is fully occupied by wishing that one was dead" [*Letters*, 128–29].) It is in the spirit of this sardonic humor that Housman's remark should be interpreted when, nine days before his death, Housman writes a letter replying to a request from R. A. Scott-James, editor of the *London Mercury*: "I am obliged by your letter, but my career and it is to be hoped my life are so near their close that it is to be hoped they will concern neither of us much longer" (*Letters*, 392).

On 24 April 1936, Housman gave his last lecture at Cambridge, and six days later he died. His ashes were buried in a churchyard in Shropshire, a county that, as he had written in a candid letter two years before his death, he did not know much about (*Letters*, 352).

Chapter Four

A Shropshire Lad

In 1896 Housman published *A Shropshire Lad*, one of the most widely admired books of poetry written in English in the nineteenth century. Reportedly, Housman had first intended to entitle the book *Poems of Terence Hearsay* to indicate that the poems are spoken by an imaginary character (Pollard, in Symons, 33). The publisher to whom Housman first submitted the collection, Macmillan, rejected it, but Kegan Paul agreed to publish it at Housman's expense. In 1898 Grant Richards published a second edition. Numerous editions followed, sales increased, and the poems' exquisite artistry, which often masks profound and complex structures of thought and feeling, has made the book permanently important. Single poems have been popular and frequently reproduced (for example, poem II, "Loveliest of trees" and poem LXII, "Terence, this is stupid stuff"), and the quality, structure, and coherence of the book as a whole have attracted scholarly and critical admiration.[1]

I. "1887"

The Golden Jubilee was a national celebration of Queen Victoria's fiftieth year on the throne, and Housman imagines what he did not in fact see—a local celebration in Shropshire, with flaming beacons and patriotic songs. Satirical use of the title of the national anthem, "God Save the Queen," had been common in popular poetry and songs of political protest for at least a century before Housman wrote "1887." Men of the Fifty-third Regiment (recruits from Shropshire) are depicted naively singing "God Save the Queen" while the speaker thinks of the young men who died serving the queen in war; if the young men here imitate their fathers, and serve the queen obediently, they too are likely to die though "God will save the Queen." The bitterness in the critical treatment of the queen's foreign wars, and in the satire of propaganda and patriotic ceremony, are handled so skillfully that some uncritical readers mistook the superficial jingoism which the poem ridicules for a positive theme, as if the poem or poet endorsed such attitudes.[2] Among others, however, Page (Page, 192–93) points out the poem's ironies and its bitterness, and B. J. Leggett observes that this poem "begins by contrasting the mood of optimism which characterized England in the 1880's with the more somber reflections of one who is unable to share that faith."[3]

Cleanth Brooks rightly pointed out (in 1959) that at the line, "Themselves they could not save," the "irony achieves a sort of climax."[4] Brooks also points out that Frank Harris—"exactly the sort of man that Housman would abominate"—once reported that Housman claimed that he "never intended to poke fun . . . at patriotism" in this poem, but that he meant "sincerely" that "if English men breed as good men as their fathers, then God will save the Queen." But Brooks is surely right to be suspicious of the anecdote. I would add that it is not surprising that the Professor of Latin would deny an intention publicly to mock the queen or her causes. Further, what Housman would *state* his intention to be might be very different from what the poem actually says and implies. The portrayal of the naive celebration among the patriotic people and the recognition of the horrible certainty of numerous deaths among them are quite clear in the poem.

The poem's artistry includes subtle use of imagery: for example, in the first stanza the phrase "From Clee to heaven" suggests the idea that the monarch is a link between earth and heaven. The marchlike rhythm of the language, most clear in the second stanza, is obviously appropriate to the military subject. In the third stanza, the first reversed foot (trochee) in the poem appears, adding rhythmical emphasis to the word "Now." The fact that Housman's intimate friend Moses Jackson left for India in 1887 may or may not be relevant to the reference to Asia in the fifth stanza, but imperial campaigns—including the annexing of Burma to the British Empire in 1885—surely are. The reference to the Nile involves the fact that Britain occupied Egypt in 1882. The poem's ironies are intensified by the inclusion of tombstones and the reference to the "dead" in a poem that (on its surface) pretends to celebrate war.

II. "Loveliest of trees"

This poem very clearly continues the theme of death, raised in poem I, but in a different frame of reference. The first line ends with the word *now*, which (simple as it is) becomes important in other poems in this collection (see, e.g., XXIV). The related themes of dying and of intense concentration upon the present moment appear also in the imagery of the season, of bloom, and of Easter. The word *Now* in the second stanza joins it with the first, even as the same word joins poems I and II. The second stanza, however, is entirely without imagery, presenting numerical counting only. The mechanical regularity of the meter in the fourth line of this stanza matches musically the bare regularity implied by the enumeration. The third stanza gathers together the "bloom" and "woodland" and "cherry" from the first stanza with the number "fifty" of the second stanza, to produce a coherent response—an indulgence, now, in beauty.

The connotations of Easter, of course, contradict the connotations of "snow"—the one implies rebirth, the other death. The fact that the liveliness of youth will *not* return contradicts the conventional content of the Easter symbolism, and likewise the theme of the seasons. Human need is here opposed to both the content of religious myth and (no less) the observable nature of the world.

It is important to recognize that this poem is a soliloquy spoken by a character very different from the poet: the poem's speaker is 20, and the poet is 36.[5] While the poem's speaker is reduced to simplicity of statement and poignant feeling, as he walks about in the woodland, the professor of Latin was busy in his urban and urbane setting, writing some of the finest works of verbal art and (in his prose) some of the best polemical art of the century. Leggett emphasizes that the poem dramatizes the persona's realization of his own mortality, and of universal mortality, and with it the intensified realization of the ephemeral beauty of the natural life, here and now.[6] Regrettably, Leggett joins that accurate perception with an attempt to deny the philosophical content of Housman's poetry; the Epicurean—and more precisely Cyrenaic—quality of the thought is evident enough. Early reviewers of *A Shropshire Lad* perceived the intellectual implications of the book very clearly, as Louise Imogen Guiney, for example, observed in 1897 that "Mr. Housman shows himself a thinker and a fine red-flag pessimist. It is a pity that he should be, in general, so shy of passing for the philosopher he is" (Gardner, 72).

III. "The Recruit"

This poem is written with remarkable skill, using the rhyme scheme of a ballad stanza (*a b c b*) with two important differences: all of the lines consist of three metrical feet (rather than the four required in the first and third lines of a traditional ballad), and while the first and third lines do not rhyme (as traditionally in a ballad stanza they do not), they are matched here in a different way: all of the first and third lines end on unaccented syllables ("feminine endings," to use the traditional term), whereas the rhymed lines end on accented syllables ("masculine endings").

The poem is a dramatic monologue, a speech spoken by an army recruiter to young men in Ludlow. Like "1887," this poem adopts an apparent rhetoric of military and patriotic enthusiasm, precisely to undermine it and to voice the opposite feelings. Poems and songs of protest about military recruitment had long been part of folk tradition. In Housman's poem, the recruiter begins by encouraging the men to enlist, on the grounds that whether they return to Ludlow on a Sunday or a Monday, they will be treated as conquering heroes. The fourth stanza, however, without the recruiter's intent, raises a morbid subject that destroys the power of his patriotic rhetoric: he indicates that whether they come home as heroes "Or come not home at all," they will be remembered. The next stanza admits that if they lie dead on foreign ground, the hearts of their friends will suffer great and permanent sorrow; the optimism has dissolved, and the prospect of being remembered by friends (which had been part of the enthusiastic appeal) has become mournful and morbid, as the last stanza's melancholy close makes painfully clear.

IV. "Reveille"

The coherence of *A Shropshire Lad* grows stronger as this poem, like "1887" and "The Recruit," begins with a voice of apparent optimism and a call to vigorous action, and then ends with an unwilling admission of a morbid truth. Again the context is war, because the reveille is the waking of soldiers, who are summoned to rise and move onward. The last stanza, however, moves beyond the particular reference to consider human beings as a mixture of clay and blood, the clay remaining as a dead body while the warm blood of a breathing person impels movement and liveliness; but life is short, breath does not last long, and the long sleep of death is (despite the speaker's effort at optimism in the beginning of the poem) memorably stated in the poem's final line. Despite the clear melancholy and sorrow, some readers of the poem have (like some readers of "1887") accepted the patriotic rhetoric as if it were sincere or naive (see Jebb, 84). Such a reading misses the critical content of Housman's poem.

V. "Oh see how thick the goldcup flowers"

This poem is an outstanding example of Housman's expert poetic craftsmanship. The poem's eight-line stanzas rhyme *a b a b c d e d*: that is, the second four-line unit within each stanza is partly out of rhyme in comparison with the first four-line unit within each stanza. Progressively as the poem goes along, the two speakers whose dialogue makes up the poem are out of agreement, and it is in the latter portion of each stanza that the two voices disagree; in this way, the versification and the content of the dialogue both portray a falling out of concord. The use of the form of dialogue, too, emphasizes the difference between the two speakers. Likewise, by portraying the two persons as fallible and disagreeing people, the dialogical form emphasizes their distance from the reader—*any* reader—of the poem.

The theme of parting is repeated here from earlier poems: the "goodbye" that ends the poem recalls the first line of III ("The Recruit")—"Leave your home behind, lad." Poem IV ("Reveille") also presents an injunction to go. The theme of mortality from I and II is raised again here in V, as in the second stanza's reflection that "the world is old"; even if "What flowers to-day" does "flower to-morrow" (and the poem suggests that it may not), it will "never" be "good as new": decay is (as in Lucretius) the way of things.

VI. "When the lad for longing sighs"

All of the words of this compressed little poem are monosyllabic with a few exceptions—"longing," "Maiden," "Lovers," and "forlorn." This simplicity of diction is characteristic of Housman, coinciding as it does with considerable complexity of effect. The plot of the poem involves a confusion of love and malice or harm—the lad who sighs for love, lying at death's door, flourishes when the maiden lies down forlorn; he is well at her expense. The commercial metaphor ("Lovers' ill are all to buy. . . . Buy them, buy them") recalls *Goblin Market* by Christina Rossetti, a poet whom Housman admired. This language clearly suggests an exchange (in this case, an exchange of suffering), but it may also imply that the conventionalized image of a mute, pale, sorrowing lover has something of an advertisement about it, with harmful consequences: to accept ("buy") such representations or poses is to risk lying down, "forlorn," in the end. The dualized pairs—buy and sell, well and forlorn, lad and maiden—remain opposed (rather than resolved or reconciled) at the poem's end, helping to account for the considerable tension that the poem sustains: the contradictions survive, rather than disappearing (as in sentimentalized love poetry) into a happy illusion at the end.

VII. "When smoke stood up from Ludlow"

Like VI, this is a poem of two voices in conflict: the poem's speaker
blithely sets out to plough a field (a recurrent metaphor for the ordinary
work of living); a blackbird speaks in stanza three, advising the ploughman to "lie down" because rising to work is, ultimately, futile. According
to the voice of the blackbird, though a person rises to struggle a thousand mornings, he will die at last ("lie down" in another sense).
Recognition of mortality and futility is represented as wisdom; again, a
hedonistic imperative emerges from the vantage of philosophical materialism as in "Loveliest of trees." In the fourth stanza, the ploughman kills
the bird with a stone, thus rejecting the pessimism and attempting
(fruitlessly, as it turns out) to silence the dark feelings that the voice of
the bird has awakened. This action furnishes a metapoetic metaphor, and
others are to follow to a like effect in *A Shropshire Lad*: Housman's poem
depicts a hostile and violent reaction to songs (poems) that painfully
remind people of their absolute mortality. To sing of an atheistic resigna-
tion is to incur the danger of violence.

The last two stanzas show, however, that this effort to silence the
voice of futility (which is the voice of the reminder of mortality) is itself
futile: the blackbird's song arises *within* the poem's speaker, though
against his will; his thoughts and feelings return to the advice to "lie
down" because "The road one treads to labour / Will lead one home to
rest." That beautifully ambivalent statement suggests at once a welcome
rest after toil, but (contradictorily, and more finally) death.

Like VI, this poem uses the rhyme scheme as a metaphor of conflict
and disjunction: as in a traditional, four-line ballad stanza, lines one and
three are out of rhyme; the added fifth line closes each stanza with a couplet, and the sense of finality is strengthened by the echo in line five of
both lines two and four. In the music of the poem, discord is followed by
an emphatic closure that mirrors the content of the dark song of the
blackbird.

VIII. "Farewell to barn and stack and tree"

This poem represents the theme of mortality in an entirely different way:
the poem is a dramatic monologue, a speech spoken by a character (in
this case, a fratricide) to another who is present but whose voice we do
not hear. "Terence" in the first stanza is a vestige of Housman's original
plan, which was to produce a volume entitled *Poems of Terence Hearsay*; we
will see Terence again in LXII, where the metapoetic theme returns in

another poem about poetry. Here, the unnamed speaker, clearly a friend of Terence, tells him that he is departing from the region (the land around the Severn River) and that he will never return; he has killed his brother Maurice with a knife, and he now flees. The poem does not proceed to any resolution but simply contrasts the desperation and emptiness of the fugitive's future with the strength, love, and sociability represented by races on the green which Terence can continue to experience. This is one among several poems about exiles, outcasts, and fugitives, in which alienation and vulnerability are rendered in narratives of crime. In poems that he did not publish, including the poem on the persecution of Oscar Wilde, apparent reference to homosexual love provides a vehicle for such narratives of isolation; here, the entirely unexplained fratricide is the poem's example. The parallel with the story of Abel and Cain was noted by "R. T. R." in an article of 1942–43, and then again by Leggett in 1970.[7]

The farewell theme is of course an echo of the theme of departures and good-byes as in III and IV; the first stanza's reference to coming home no more recalls the third stanza of "1887." Where here the "blood has dried," in the second stanza of V "blood runs gold"; *this* poem makes disturbingly explicit (and criminally violent) the issue—death—whose latent presence in the earlier poem had contributed to its melancholy music.

IX. "On moonlit heath and lonesome bank"

Forty years after the first publication of *A Shropshire Lad*, Housman wrote that "the best review I ever saw of my poems was by Hubert Bland the Socialist," and in that review Bland said of this poem that it is, "if not the best, . . . the one most characteristic of Mr. Housman's genius" (Gardner, 59–60). Killing, which had been treated in terms of war in poems I, III, and IV, is implicitly compared with the ordinary crime of murder in VIII, and it is represented in connection with execution by hanging in IX. In the second stanza, the apparent innocence and calm of the pastoral language about a "careless shepherd" keeping "flocks by moonlight" is violently undermined by the reference of that metaphor; as a footnote printed with the poem in the first edition indicates, hanging a person at a gallows, in chains, was formerly called "keeping sheep by moonlight." The careless shepherd is, hence, an insidious figure from this point of view: a person who has authority, and who does not care. The use of an apparently lovely image on the surface (shepherd, flocks, moonlight) to present in veiled form a disturbing action or meaning is characteristic of Housman's poetry.

The third stanza indicates that "They hang us now in Shrewsbury jail," whereas in the past they hanged us at the gallows on the heath; but still "they" hang "us." The identification of the poem's speaker with the victim is important in the emotion and meaning conveyed by this monologue. The fourth stanza suggests that a young man who is now about to be hanged is likely to have been a better person, under better circumstances, than most people who are now comfortable outside jails. The point is critical: circumstances determine character and action; external conditions, including chance, determine who is criminal and who is not. But for reasons that are thus merely conditional, the young man "now" in Shrewsbury jail will be killed.

Amidst the high seriousness of this moral and social issue, Housman introduces grim humor, as with the pun on the word "ring" in stanza 5, when the clocks that will sound the hour for the killing of the young man are said to "ring / A neck". The poem's conclusion returns to the parallel between the practice of hanging people, as it was done a century ago, and this new execution that will take place tomorrow. There is class conflict ("they" hang "us"), and there is a sociological point of view (circumstances determine character and acts), and there is a profoundly skeptical vision introduced by the poem: what endures over time is not truth, but cruelty, crime determined by surrounding conditions, and the violence of retribution which is (according to the fifth stanza) ungodly.

X. "March"

The title of this poem refers (obviously) to the month, but the presence of one clear pun in the immediately preceding poem suggests that the word *march* may have some military echoes here, in addition to its obvious seasonal meaning. Likewise, the fourth stanza in IX suggests that the phrase "should be" in X might well be taken with some irony: IX suggests that justice and fairness have nothing to do with the way things actually turn out, and X lets us hear the voice of a young man who still retains some naive sense of what "should be."

The astrological imagery in the poem's first stanza ("the silver Pair," "the Ram") is of course classical, providing a metaphor for the passing of time. Here, however, the world and its cycles of time and seasons are portrayed as "the rusted wheel of things," which suggests a very different attitude from the conventionally happy images of poems on the springtime. This portrayal of destructive futility, where conventional lyrics of springtime had put naive gladness, becomes an important theme in *A Shropshire Lad*: the pessimistic metaphor of life as a treadmill in poem LV is an example. The theme of "lovers" is also developed darkly and ironically in subsequent poems, including poem XI, which follows immediately.

XI. "On your midnight pallet lying"

In this poem, the speaker's request that his lover undo the door at midnight is accompanied by a traditional opposition of light and dark: the light has been "wasted" as in the "Nurse's Song" in William Blake's *Songs of Experience*, and sighing should cease in the dark. As in Blake's poem, however, night is associated with death: the sorrow of the lover, and all sighing, will end in the dark of death, and for that reason the indulgence of love is sought now. The phrase, "since I go to-morrow," takes on multiple meanings: besides the general condition (death as impending departure for everyone), the context established by earlier poems including "The Recruit" (III) suggests that the speaker is going to war, and the imagery of the anticipated grave in a distant land, in the last stanza, is associated with the tombstones in foreign lands that are mentioned in "1887" (I). The poem thus *seems* to have an abstract or universal reference to death as the "far dwelling" to which the speaker travels, but the book's first poem identifies the imperial wars during Victoria's reign as the particular occasion of killing and dying against which the poem voices its protest.

XII. "When I watch the living meet"

The "house of dust" where the speaker's stay shall be long is the ordinary ground, smothered in darnel, mentioned in the immediately preceding poem: the second stanza states a resolution to remember this destination, while temporarily the heats of emotions are strong. The "pageant" that files through the street is temporary, even momentary, and only for a little while can the speaker lodge here: as in poem XI, there are three levels of reference in this passage, including the superficial story of a temporary lodger who must soon leave, a soldier soon to be shipped to the foreign war, and the universal condition of mortal human beings. The satire of nationalism begun in I ("1887") is continued here, where the dead are called the "nation that is not," and the grim emptiness of dead lovers, suggested already by poem XI, is indicated even more bitterly here where the corpse of a bridegroom is said (truly enough) to be indifferent to the corpse of the bride. Clearly, the ancient themes of lyrical poetry—*eros* and *thanatos* (love and death)—are situated in the story of the lad recruited from Shropshire for the Victorian imperial wars.

XIII. "When I was one-and-twenty"

The artistry of this poem has helped to make it one of the more frequently reprinted poems from *A Shropshire Lad*: its eight-line stanzas, having three accents per line, are organized in a distinctive way that Housman will use several times, in this book and in others: in each stanza, lines two and four rhyme, and then lines six and eight rhyme; in contrast, the odd-numbered lines do not rhyme at all, but each ends with an unaccented syllable (i.e., a "feminine" ending). The alternation of accented ("masculine") and unaccented endings is a device for patterns of sound, like rhyme, but allowing greater variety.

Here the love theme is again treated critically by the use of imagery of wealth (money and jewels, "paid" and "sold"). The poem uses the device of a speaker quoting another speaker to exhibit the problem of different viewpoints, and it uses the change of one single person's viewpoint, over time, to suggest an even more powerful reason for skepticism. Though one *likes* to recite confidently "'tis true, 'tis true," the poem gives us reason to reflect that any state of mind is temporary and limited by personal viewpoint, rather than "true" in the dogmatic sense.

XIV. "There pass the careless people"

This poem's central stanza connects its subject matter to the immediately preceding poem by stating the folly of giving one's heart away. The first stanza of this poem connects it with poem XII, because XII and XIV are both about the passage of people down the road, in contrast to the alienated speaker, a bystander whose buried and secret feelings are hidden more deeply than the ocean floor. The ironic use of the phrase, "World without end," connects with the use of "doomsday" in the final stanza to apply religious vocabulary to an entirely mortal, human, and even (as in stanza three) sexual subject matter.

XV. "Look not in my eyes, for fear"

This remarkable poem combines a simplicity on its surface with a complexity of implications: every word and every sentence are unmistakably clear, but several layers of meaning are achieved at once. The theme of love as failure, associated with loss and destruction, is here combined with mythic analogy (the Narcissus myth, told in the second stanza) and with classical materialism (like that of Democritus, Epicurus, and Lucretius): a dead person is organic matter recycled as a plant. The deceptive relativity of viewpoints (as in poem XIII) is conveyed in the opening image of eyes as mirrors; this theme is then joined with the problem of destructive love (as in X, XII, and XIII) and with naturalistic mortality in contrast to the illusory promises of religion, as the ironic treatment of "world without end" suggests in XIV.

The versification of this poem is also artful: it is like the eight-line stanzas of XIII, except that this poem's stanzas add one foot to each line (making four-accent lines, whereas XII used three), and these stanzas add an additional rhyme by rhyming the odd-numbered lines as well as the even. The result is an amplification of the earlier poem's structure.

XVI. "It nods and curtseys and recovers"

This poem very clearly links itself to the preceding poem, presenting an image of a plant growing from the grave of a person: here, it is not a jonquil but a nettle, but (as in XV) the death is caused by a false and futile love. The image of lovers' graves is repeated here from poem XII; further, graves and tombs appear in the poems that treat war critically (including I ["1887"]), so that a thematic continuity is achieved, linking the themes of love and death. Whereas the image of hanging in poem IX refers to the execution of a criminal, the repetition of that image here involves suicide (very obviously), a topic that will also return in subsequent poems.

The poem's two stanzas are traditional ballad stanzas (quatrains in which lines of four feet and three feet alternate, with alternating rhyme) except that Housman has added two sound effects to develop a musical theme: the odd lines have "feminine" endings and the even lines have "masculine" endings (as in poem XIII), and Housman has added rhyme to the odd lines (whereas most traditional ballad stanzas do not rhyme the odd lines).

XVII. "Twice a week the winter through"

The context shifts, in this poem, from classical mythology to the (fictitious) setting in nineteenth-century Shropshire: the speaker observes that young people took soccer seriously, in its season, as if it were somehow important rather than merely a game (and therefore by definition purposeless); then the season of another sport arrived, and *it* was taken seriously, as people attempted to be happy; the last stanza then bitterly reflects on how trivial the amusements are which represent life, as opposed to the inevitability of death. The poem thus uses the example of sports to represent the futility of meaningless activity about which people somehow manage, foolishly, to get excited during the brief interval before they are bones in a graveyard. Sports are here a metaphor for conventional life, with *its* hurried, strenuous, but ultimately meaningless exertion, and with the delusion that these exertions are somehow worth concern. Later in *A Shropshire Lad*, this metaphor is developed in more complex ways, as in poem XIX, "To an Athlete Dying Young," where the futility of exertion (or cheering) in sports is compared to the futility (and cheering) in war. In both cases, sports as a metaphor of meaninglessness is linked with the futility of a deluded life that ends, absolutely, in ordinary death.

XVIII. "Oh, when I was in love with you"

The speaker of XVIII, like the speaker of XIII, furnishes an instance of a change of viewpoint: in stanza one, there are love, bravery, and wonderful behavior; then, in the way of things, all of this gladness passes away; and (in a way that is characteristic of the multiple meanings of *A Shropshire Lad*) the reflection becomes general or even universal ("nothing will remain").

The versification of this poem is the same as that of XVI—two ballad stanzas with added rhyme for the odd lines. This musical parallelism highlights the thematic similarity, involving temporality, loss, and inevitable change and decay.

XIX. "To an Athlete Dying Young"

The first stanza states a memory of happy crowds carrying a victorious athlete on their shoulders; stanza two compares the carrying of the same person's corpse, in a casket, to the graveyard. As so often in *A Shropshire Lad*, the topic is generalized or universalized, rather than concentrated on this particular person's story: the road to the graveyard is "the road all runners come." Like poem XVII, then, this poem begins with an ironic reflection on the futility of racing as a metaphor for the futility of conventional lives. The speaker indicates that illusion ("glory") does not last long; neither does life itself. The belief that athletic success is somehow glorious is undermined by the reflection that the garland of victory is reduced to nothingness even more quickly than is the ornamental garland of a girl. In its context in the collection, the poem suggests an analogy between athletic endeavor and war: the implication is that sports are a state-sponsored rehearsal for war, and that sports fans are practicing the political attitudes that will be necessary to support an imperialistic war: they are cheering for their side.

XX. "Oh fair enough are sky and plain"

This poem develops the theme of illusion by returning to the image of mirror reflection from poem XV: in this instance, the reflections of objects on the surfaces of rivers and ponds are said to be more beautiful than any objects that actually exist in the world. In *The Picture of Dorian Gray*, Oscar Wilde (to whom Housman sent a copy of *A Shropshire Lad*) had used the image of a painting in a similar way: a visual representation of things (as in a painting or a reflection on water) is produced as an analogy for the equally artificial imagery that we call consciousness. In the classical literature of skepticism, the analogy between human perception and two-dimensional representations is used to cast all human thought and belief into doubt, because there are important differences between things and two-dimensional images of things. In nineteenth-century literature, the function and meaning of art are sometimes explored by the same analogy (as, for example, in works by Wilde): in this poem, the false beauty on a two-dimensional surface suggests that art (including traditional poetry) may distort things by creating falsely beautiful impressions. The fact that the speaker of this poem looks at those images on the water's surface because he is thinking of drowning himself returns to the theme of suicide raised in poem XVI. The speaker indicates that he does not kill himself, but only because he recognizes the equal meaninglessness of the image in the water and the gazer at the image, which reciprocally produce only illusion. Neither fully appreciates the nothingness of the other.

XXI. "Bredon Hill"

Here the problem of death returns but in a more complicated narrative: the pastoral prettiness of conventional lyrics, including larks, thyme, and spring, is contrasted with churchgoing: first, a young woman is summoned to church on an ordinary Sunday, thus disrupting the lovers' "happy" moment together; a wedding is pictured as another instance of proceeding to the church; then, the woman dies, and the carrying of her coffin to the churchyard, followed by mourners, is another example of going to church. Finally, the speaker of the poem contemplates his own impending death: thus, by the end of the poem, everyone has gone to church (that is, died), and the illusion of "happy" time has been replaced by the morbid but inevitable futility and desolation of dying. Religion (the church, obviously) is a symbol of the darkening and destruction of human desire and life.

As the treatment of imagery in poem XX suggests that representation is often false (and implicitly, representations in art are often false), this poem's parody of pastoral imagery involves an implicit critique of conventionally pretty pastoral poetry: as in poem IX, where pastoral imagery (there, a shepherd) is similarly used, futile dying, without the illusory consolations of imaginary immortality, contributes to the undermining of the traditional deceptions of religion and art alike.

XXII. "The street sounds to the soldiers' tread"

The return here to the topic of soldiers involves the associated imagery of a procession and a spectator, as in poems XII and XIV. Alienation (one of the most widespread themes in nineteenth-century literature) is the conceptual focus, because the soldier and the speaker are said to look at one another only for a moment, and without any communication of any thoughts that they might have. The central stanza suggests that the world is a vast emptiness, with widely separated people on it, who can (at best) mutely wish each other well without any real understanding of who they might be. At the same time, as in "1887," "The Recruit," and "Reveille," the dispersal of British soldiers to foreign lands in Victoria's imperial wars of colonial conquest is represented in terms of the human loss undergone at home.

XXIII. "The lads in their hundreds to Ludlow come in for the fair"

Immediately following that poem about soldiers, the first stanza of this poem, referring to young men who will never grow old, continues the theme. Stalwart, brave, and handsome, many of these young men will die, and no one knows which. The third stanza's statement about the road down which the men depart, never to return, recalls earlier poems (including VII, XI, and XIX) in its threefold use of the image of the road: the literal road down which the young men go, the journeying of soldiers to their distant military destination, and the linear progress of all persons to their graves. The last stanza uses the degrading image of money, as XIII had done, but here it is not "love" but rather the young men themselves that are degraded to the status of money: the young men are not even considered as people, under that metaphor, but rather animated coins, which are instruments of somebody's profit-making schemes. The implication about the British colonial wars is obvious.

The versification of this poem is both unusual and strikingly expressive: the poem consists of four quatrains, with alternating rhyme among lines of five feet each. These would be elegiac stanzas (the meter, for example, of Thomas Gray's "Elegy Written in a Country Churchyard"), traditionally used for meditations on mortality; but elegiac stanzas use iambic pentameter, and these pentameter lines are iambic only in the first foot of each line; all other feet are lengthened to anapests. The result is a musical achievement of some complexity, because the elegiac stanza and its associations are suggested (especially because each line begins in the traditional iambic measure), but then a more jolly, swinging rhythm is used, contrasting the sound of a dancing-hall song with the morbidity of a meditation on death.

XXIV. "Say, lad, have you things to do?"

Versification in this poem also adds musical power to its voicing of the urgency that results from awareness of impending death: the poem's three stanzas are tetrameter quatrains in alternating rhyme, but the lines are headless: that is, each line starts and stops on an accent. The lines are iambic (minus the initial unaccented syllable) or trochaic (plus an additional accent at the end). The effect is a headlong tumble down shortened lines, which beautifully matches the urgency of the repeated imperative, "Quick then" and "Quick . . . now's your time."

XXV. "This time of year a twelvemonth past"

This poem is a story of a death, in a traditional ballad stanza (with added rhyme in the odd lines). The speaker says that he and Fred had fought; Fred won; Rose Harland walked with the winner; but now Fred is dead and Rose Harland walks with the speaker; one living man is better than many dead. The harsh irony of the story includes the fact that the traditional happy ending (a lover winning the beloved) comes to look meaningless: who wins or loses, who is loved or not, even who desires what, are momentary and trivial in comparison with the enduring emptiness of the buried clay that was once a person and the buried clay that all of the persons shall permanently become.

XXVI. "Along the field as we came by"

In two stanzas of tetrameter couplets, this poem tells an analogous story: a year ago, the speaker and his lover walked past a tree, apparently planning to be married; the tree tells a stone that, in time, the woman will be dead and the man will have another lover. In the second stanza, that is exactly what has happened, but the speaker fears that the tree (the sound of whose leaves means nothing to him) may be telling his new lover the same thing that it had told him, which is the same thing that poem XXV tells in its story: what may look like permanent love is a momentary alignment on a road, to be succeeded (with grim certainty) by death, faithlessness, and impoverishment of meaning and human value.

XXVII. "Is my team ploughing"

Housman came to think of this poem as one of his best (Richards, 8; Haber 1966, 144), and his reasons are likely to have involved the poem's superb craftsmanship and his characteristic combination of simple diction with complex ranges of meaning. Superficially, like the two preceding poems this imaginary dialogue of a dead man with his friend tells a story of faithless love: the reassuring friend who is alive has become the lover of the dead man's sweetheart, as we learn in the last stanza. In previous stanzas, he assures the dead man that his lover lies down easily (not weeping), and (under the guise of wishing his dead friend peace) advises him to sleep and ask no more hard questions; of course his wish to silence the questions is born of his guilty consciousness that he has become the lover of the dead man's girl, and this guilt is masked as compassion.

Like poem III ("The Recruit"), this poem consists of quatrains in which the second and fourth lines rhyme (as in a traditional ballad stanza) while the first and third do not; but (also as in the case of poem III) the first and third lines are matched in a different way: they have feminine endings, whereas the second and fourth lines have masculine endings. Finally, like the lines in poem III but in contrast to a traditional ballad, *all* of the lines consist of three metrical feet (three accents). The metrical art in this poem is yet more careful and intricate, however: all of the stanzas spoken by the dead man begin with lines of five syllables, whereas all of the other lines in the poem (including, obviously, the first lines of stanzas spoken by the falsely reassuring friend) contain six syllables. The effect of this truncation is to impart urgency to the dead man's questions by means of abruptness in sound as well as meaning.

The first two stanzas suggest that the work of the dead man (plowing) goes on, though others now do it; the cyclical, repetitious absurdity of football, as in poem XVII and poem XIX, returns here in stanzas three and four, indicating that the conventional form of play which had been his also continues, though others do it; and the remaining stanzas show that the act of love he had enjoyed with his sweetheart is also repeated without him, as another person does it. Unique persons (the poem shows) die, but the merely physical motions of life go on, as people replace one another, just as (to borrow a metaphor from later poems in the collection) leaves on trees are ephemeral but new leaves emerge in new seasons, as nature's cycles carry on without us.

XXVIII. "The Welsh Marches"

"Marches" are border regions: this poem deepens the antiwar theme of the collection by historicizing it, referring to ancient border wars while internalizing the conflict and the horror of war as an inescapable suffering inside a person as well as between persons and nations. As John Bayley has written, the speaker's "heart, like the marches, is the scene of age-old war, oppression, hatred between sex and race" (Bayley, 158). The first stanza treats the island location of Shrewsbury, on the river Severn, with its bridges connecting it to both sides, as a site of conflict on the margin between warring regions. The second stanza presents daylight and night in the metaphor of conqueror (England) and conquered (Wales): the war is conflict in nature, and not only nations. The speaker thinks of his ancestor suffering at the convergence of conflicting forces— love (the marriage bed) and killing (the "vanquished bled"). The fourth stanza refers to the rape of a woman by an invading Saxon warrior: the present speaker is the offspring of past atrocity. Though that particular battle is long past, its conflicts survive inside the speaker: only death, the lyric concludes, will end the torment of internal conflict that the speaker suffers, as he embodies within himself the warring opposites that are represented emotionally (as hatred) and historically (as conquering Saxons). The poem ends in a death wish: only his annihilation will bring peace.

This poem's achievements include the extension of the war theme (or the antiwar theme) over a larger historical range and the strengthening of the connection between national war and personal experience. As earlier poems had united a literal parting of a particular lad from his lover with a metaphorical representation of human mortality, this poem represents a historical continuity of insoluble conflict, metaphorically (one war of conquest resembles another) and literally (the natural process of genetics produces the speaker who is the offspring of ancient wartime rape). The brutality and horror of the past survive, repeated, here and now.

XXIX. "The Lent Lily"

The title of this poem contains one of Housman's infrequent puns: the lily blooms at Lent, but it cannot be kept. The superb and biting irony of the poem involves the traditional (even ancient) springtime call to ramble among the blossoms, gathering flowers: the primroses (stanza one) and the windflower (stanza two). The lily of Lent, however, is said to die on Easter day: the popular (religious) fiction of rebirth and immortality is contradicted by the natural fact of death. The poem's presentation of the *carpe diem* theme may at first seem to be classical (the Latin poet Horace, of course, being the source of the phrase *carpe diem*), but it is decidedly *not* classical: the poem refers to the practice of girls' going maying (like Robert Herrick's "Corinna's Going a-Maying"), and ends as Herrick's poem does by suggesting that people should seek their pleasure now *because* all living things die. But Housman adds what Herrick does not: a satirical contrast of the Christian figment of immortality (as in the fiction about Christ's *rising from* the dead on Easter) with the pagan (and Epicurean) recognition that life is short and beauty dies soon. Likewise, the religious doctrine of renunciation (during the 40 days of Lent) is contrasted with the Epicurean call to seize the brief moment of beauty while one can.

Within a year of the first appearance of *A Shropshire Lad*, Louise Imogen Guiney noticed this complex feature of the book, its sophisticated but sardonic allusion to the English *carpe diem* tradition from a more modern and philosophically materialist point of view: "Herrick's dear old May poles and wassail-cakes are fantastic as a Versailles masque beside these ugly villageous ingredients: spites, jealousies and slit throats . . . the barracks, the jail, and the hangman's rope. . . . [The] beautiful little book, on the whole, is keyed low, so low as approval of suicide, and allowance of blasphemy" (Gardner, 70).

XXX. "Others, I am not the first"

Leggett has emphasized that this is one of the poems in which the difference between the poet and the speaker is crucial: the speaker of the poem attempts to rationalize his passions, his desire, and his guilt, and to seek comfort from merely intellectual reflections about them; in contrast, the physical details—"breathless," "shiver," fire and ice in the "reins" (i.e., the loins or the physical location of passion)—undermine these rationalizations. What the poem reveals is *not* what the speaker says about taking comfort from the fact that many people suffer similar feelings, or about finding comfort in the prospect of peace after death; instead, "the poem reveals the inadequacy of the intellect, the domination of the feelings" (Leggett 1978, 50–51). Further, following "The Lent Lily," this poem continues the theme of opposing impulses toward conventional and moralistic renunciation (as in Lent and in religious doctrine generally) and the realities of physical passion and physical death. The continuity over history among people who are temporarily passionate but permanently mortal also develops the theme from "The Welsh Marches," where interior conflict inside the speaker is also assimilated with the materialistic continuity of the dead and dying generations. The thematic complexity, achieved with deceptively simple language, was hard-won: Haber reports that 11 of the poem's 16 lines were revised from the initial version that Housman wrote, and that most of the lines were rewritten substantially.

XXXI. "On Wenlock Edge the wood's in trouble"

This poem's development of these same themes is elaborate and beautiful, though compressed into short and lucid form. Just as "The Welsh Marches" had assimilated the ancient wars of Saxons and Celts with the present internal conflict of the speaker, this poem identifies the thoughts and the blood of the ancient Roman who occupied this territory with the modern Englishman's thoughts and feelings. According to the classical materialism of the Roman poet Lucretius *and* according to the modern science in which Housman had expressed interest ("it is up to Science to show what is the reality of the world" [quoted by Graves 1979, 48]), the matter that made up the Roman *is* the matter that makes up a person now; and, further, according to Lucretius and according to modern science, human thought *is* a physical phenomenon in the physical matter of the body. As Housman does here, Lucretius uses the image of the wind as an analogy for the motion that is human thought: wind disturbs the forest as thought disturbs the brain. Here, "the old wind in the old anger" assimilates *objects* with *emotion* naturalistically.

This conceptual content was clearly understood by early reviewers of *A Shropshire Lad*: an unsigned review in *Academy* (8 October 1898), for example, writes thus of "the philosophy with which [Housman] encounters his 'lost content'": "Man is thrown together from pre-existent elements, and dislimns like a summer cloud, again to be brought together in fresh combinations. We are swayed by ancestral passions, and our ancestors live in us again. . . . It is . . . the philosophy of Ecclesiastes . . . *plus* the doctrine of heredity" (Gardner, 83–84).

Coherently with the volume as a whole, this poem presents the historical continuity of past and present and the material continuity among generations of mortal people in terms of trouble: in the third stanza, what thoughts do is to *hurt* the person who has them, as the storm damages the woods. The organism called "man" was never peaceful (stanza four); and like other poems in *A Shropshire Lad*, including the immediately preceding poem, this one ends with an image of annihilation as the only possible peace.

XXXII. "From far, from eve and morning"

This poem develops the preceding poem's materialism, with direct statements about "the stuff of life" that "blew hither" to make up the body of the speaker, but which will (as in Lucretius's materialism) "disperse apart" in the wind, to make up some other physical object (Bayley points out the analogy with Lucretius's line, "pereat dispersa per auras," [perishes dispersed through the air]—Bayley, 34; and see Haber 1966, 163). The recognition of the brevity of life prompts a feeling of urgency, as in earlier poems, but the goal of the injunction *carpe diem* is not sexual but rather compassionate: "Take my hand quick and tell me, / What have you in your heart."

Like poem III ("The Recruit") and XIII ("When I was one-and-twenty"), this poem resembles a ballad, but all of its lines contain three metrical feet each, rather than alternating lines of four and three feet, as a ballad stanza does. The matched regularity of the poem's three stanzas represents considerable artistry, as the numerous manuscript revisions reveal (see Haber 1966, 164–66).

XXXIII. "If truth in hearts that perish"

Like Andrew Marvell's "To His Coy Mistress," this poem uses the structure of a hypothetical syllogism: in Marvell's poem, *if* we had sufficient time, the speaker would court slowly; *but* all persons die soon; *therefore* seize the brief moment of love and beauty. Here, in Housman's poem, *if* truth could influence some power that ruled the world, and *if* meaning or thought could save anything, then "you should live forever." *But* "all is idle": thought, truth, meaning, desire, and effort are futile, no one does live forever, and *therefore* the speaker says, "To this lost heart be kind." The metaphor of death as the end of a journey, where only indifference is found, returns from earlier poems (including VII, XI, XIX, and XXIII). In contrast to the next poem ("The New Mistress"), this poem does not use the image of the journey to refer explicitly to troops in transit but rather refers directly to simple and universal death, consistently with the poems that immediately precede this one.

XXXIV. "The New Mistress"

As Chauncey Brewster Tinker pointed out 60 years ago, this poem is similar to Rudyard Kipling's *Barrack-Room Ballads* in its use of ballad rhythm to represent the voice of a soldier who goes off to war. "Lady" and "mistress" represent the queen and the empire that he serves.[8] Tinker, however, attempts to deny the obvious satire in this poem: the soldier's actual destination is not the illusion of comfort, reward, and glory to which he thinks he goes; it is, instead, the war "Where the standing line wears thinner and the dropping dead lie thick."

The poem's ballad rhythm suggests the sound of a popular song, though it is represented here in a fairly common variant form: rather than alternating lines of four and three beats, with rhyme only among the lines of three beats, the poem is printed in lines of seven beats each—exactly the same as the ballad stanza in number of syllables and in its meter and rhyme, but printed in the format of the longer line, called traditionally the "fourteener."

XXXV. "On the idle hill of summer"

In four stanzas of four lines each, with four accents per line, this poem develops the theme of the seasons (treated earlier in poems II, X, XVII, XXI, XXVII, and XXIX) in terms of soldiers and war, which was also the subject of the immediately preceding poem. The first stanza situates the speaker in the dreamy stillness of summer, but the noise of distant drums is audible. "The roads of earth" are, literally, the routes of soldiers who march off, "all to die"; but the phrase ("of earth") generalizes the meaning, as in earlier poems (including VII, XIV, XIX, and XXIII), to suggest the futile movement of all humanity toward the meaningless inertness of bleached bones (here, in stanza three; the imagery of bones is repeated from poem XVII). The irony amounting to sarcasm that appears in earlier poems in *A Shropshire Lad* reappears here (as in the line, "Lovely lads and dead and rotten"). The deceptive appeal to glory in poem III ("The Recruit") returns here, too, as the "gay" sound of bugles and fife summon the poem's speaker. Like the speaker of poem XXIII, the speaker of this poem has recognized that "None that go return again"; there is bitterness in the poem's end, therefore, as the speaker says that he, too, will march off with the others on the road to an inescapable and ultimately meaningless death.

XXXVI. "White in the moon the long road lies"

This poem presents a parody of popular songs and sentimental lyric poetry alike: the repetition within stanza one of the line, "White in the moon the long road lies," and the repetition at the poem's end of the cliché that ends the first stanza, "leads me from my love," emphasize the redundant jingling of conventional propaganda of love, just as the anti-war poems satirize the conventional propaganda of war. The repetition of "Still, still" (in stanza two) and of "Trudge on, trudge on" (stanza three) is obviously an example of imitative form, as "still" slows the line, and the word *trudge* imitates the action of trudging. The meaningless recycling of "moon" and "love" in popular songs and lyrical poetry is itself a repetition of the grim vision of the world's futile cycles which the last two stanzas state. The recycling of the matter that made a Roman in poem XXXI is combined here with the image of "the roads of earth" in XXXV, immediately preceding.[9] The return of imagery in different poems in *A Shropshire Lad* is itself another instance of the *theme* of return, as in this poem the cycles of the moon and of the round earth are used to portray an arduous journey to nowhere.

XXXVII. "As through the wild green hills of Wyre"

Here, the road in the poem's story is the actual road from Shropshire to London, as the speaker leaves his home to live in the city. His hand aches from the numerous handshakes of his departing friends, whose well-wishing the speaker remembers, and whose memory will (he says) inspire his future goodness. The land in which he will forget them, he says, is "the land where all's forgot"—a thematic repetition (like a theme in music) of the "nation that is not" from poem XII, "When I watch the living meet." The gladness of the poem's opening portion is, however, merely a momentary appearance: the deathly suggestions implicit in that thought of "the land where all's forgot" transform this literal road to the city into another metaphor for the progress to death—the handshake that was apparently benevolent was in truth "A grasp to friend me to the grave," just as (in poem XXXIII) neither love nor thought of any kind can save anyone.

The poem's tetrameter couplets (in musical contrast with the quatrains of most of the poems) recall the verse form of Marvell's "To His Coy Mistress," where the ghastly inevitability of death is also presented directly.

XXXVIII. "The winds out of the west land blow"

As in poem XXXI the wind connects the ancient Roman with the modern Englishman, here the wind connects the breathing friends in Shropshire with the speaker on his road to London: the wind has been warmed by the blood of his friends, when they breathed it before it reached him. The third stanza repeats (like a variation on a theme) the dispersal of atoms, bodies, and even human lives, from poem XXXII. The theme of futility is made explicit in stanza four, when the friends' voices are imagined sounding "down the sighing wind in vain," and when, in the final stanza, the speaker identifies himself with the wind (as bodies and lives were identified with the wind in poems XXXI and XXXII), though neither can exist for long; the world is "friendless" and the road (this poem ends on that central image, "road") is a place on which to "sigh."

This poem is pivotal in Leggett's account of the structure of *A Shropshire Lad* considered as a whole: Leggett says that the book is divided into three portions: a frame composed of the first poem and the last two poems; a section containing poems whose setting is Shropshire (poems II through XXXVII); and a section of poems whose speaker is in "exile," in London or in the course of journeying to London (poems XXXVIII to LXI). Uncertainty has dominated, among critics of the book, about whether the sequence has any such careful narrative order (see Leggett 1970, 70–78). One of the earliest reviews of *A Shropshire Lad* (the reviewer was anonymous, but probably was Annie Macdonnell) describes the unity of the volume in this way: "His book of lyrics has continuity. You can pick out a story from it, several linked dramas of the lives of Shropshire lads, the one that used his knife in anger, and stood under the shadow of the gallows, and lay long in jail; the one that went for a soldier; the one that, after his struggle for love, lay early in the churchyard. But there is no continuous narrative" (Gardner, 65).

Beyond uncertainty about whether the poems are organized to tell a coherent story in an orderly way, three points do emerge in a consensus of critical opinion: the poems have a thematic unity at least, if not necessarily a narrative unity; and some critics, including apparently the pious upholders of orthodox religious thinking, have not liked his poems' atheism, skepticism, and pessimism; for example, an anonymous reviewer in the *Guardian* in 1896 writes that Housman "is a philosopher, a disciple of Democritus, and he holds that we are not spirits as the best men have thought, but bodies impatient to be delivered of their skeleton, which he grimly calls 'the immortal part'" (Gardner, 67–68). But the artistry of his lyrics is widely admired, especially because of the apparent simplicity in the poems' surfaces coexisting with the complex and fascinating depths of feeling and thought which are masked by the apparent simplicity.

XXXIX. "'Tis time, I think, by Wenlock town"

This poem invites comparison with II, "Loveliest of trees," because the image of white blossoms as snow is repeated here in stanza one, and the theme of loss is common to them both. The second stanza of this poem treats the theme of an indifferent and humanly meaningless world, though in a remarkably sly way: the spring will not wait for the speaker to return to Shropshire, to enjoy the beauty of the season, but its white and golden flowers bloom in his absence. The poem concludes with a wish for the long survival of beauty in the flowers, though he is gone: again, the literal absence of a man on a journey is superimposed over a figurative level of meaning, wherein all persons are dying, and wherein (as in poem XXII) the best that estranged mortals can do is to wish one another well across the vast expanses of their alienation.

XL. "Into my heart an air that kills"

This poem is connected to poem XXXVIII in its imagery of the wind, and in the literal story of the Shropshire lad who has left his home to travel to the city, and in its themes as well; it also uses the same verse form, which is a traditional ballad stanza with rhyme added to lines one and three of each stanza (in addition to the traditional rhyme of lines two and four). Here, beauty that is lost actually becomes destructive: the "far country" with its "blue remembered hills" comes to the speaker in a wind that, laden with memories that are painful because of loss, "kills." The speaker's attitude is antiromantic and antisentimental: lovely memories are not wholesome, curative, or restorative, but deadly. The poem voices discontent and despair; like the sarcastic "lovely lads and dead and rotten" (in XXXV), in this poem the "happy highways" are actually an image of bitterness because they lead from the "land of lost content," the place (and the life) of happiness and of beauty to which the alienated speaker "cannot come again."

XLI. "In my own shire, if I was sad"

At home, the speaker says, he had "comforters": the sympathetic earth and the "beautiful and death–struck year" were natural companions, "bound for the same bourn as I"—and that "bourn" or end is of course annihilation in the natural way of things. That sympathy in nature, however, is a thing of the past for the young man who is now in the city (London): here, he has no such comforters, but only men who are themselves in such a bad situation that they simply cannot concern themselves with another person's plight. In the city, every person in the crowd has too much misery of his or her own to allow them to care about others' suffering. In the city, people are "Too unhappy to be kind." They are "undone with misery"; urbanization has affected people such that all they can do, now, "Is to hate their fellow man." Finally, in a direct reversal of the well-wishing in poems XXII and XXXIX, this poem observes that urbanized people "needs must" (that is, they are *caused* to) "wish you ill."

Thus, this poem raises a social issue that—like the antiwar theme in other poems in *A Shropshire Lad*—engages the book in critical commentary on its own historical time, which is, of course, the industrialized and urbanized end of the nineteenth century. *A Shropshire Lad*'s critique of the dehumanization brought about by urbanization links Housman's book to many books by his contemporaries: in *Change in the Village*, for example, George Bourne writes in a tone of loss about the folk in the villages of an older, rural England: "unawares, they lived as integral parts in the rural community," which is what the first verse paragraph of Housman's poem XLI portrays. Bourne writes of industrialization and urbanization in this way: "the coherent and self-explanatory village life

had given place to a half blind struggle of individuals against circumstances and economic processes," and this competitive life is what
Housman portrays in the poem's second verse paragraph. Likewise, in
The Wheelwright's Shop, George Sturt writes of "the death of Old England
and of the replacement of the more primitive nation by an 'organized'
modern state"; Sturt writes that "village life was dying out; intelligent
interest in the countryside was being lost; the class-war was destroying
erstwhile quiet communities," and "'the Men,' though still my friends,
as I fancied, became machine 'hands'. Unintentionally, I had made them
servants." F. R. Leavis and Denys Thompson (whose book *Culture and
Environment* quotes these passages from Bourne and Sturt) write that "we
all suffer by the loss of the organic community. . . . Sturt's villagers
expressed their human nature, they satisfied their human needs, in terms
of the natural environment; and . . . their relations with one another
constituted a human environment." Not only social critics, but writers of
imaginative literature in Housman's lifetime tended to develop these
ideas frequently: for example, D. H. Lawrence writes that "industrial
England blots out the agricultural England. One meaning blots out
another. The new England blots out the old England. And the continuity is not organic, but mechanical" and "the industrial problem arises
from the base forcing of all human energy into a competition of mere
acquisition."[10] The story told in *A Shropshire Lad* is a story of the loss of
village life amid natural environs, and the loss of comradeship in the
"human environment" that such life involved. Imperialism (including its
foreign wars and its commercial motives) and urbanization (with stan-
dardized lives of competition and hostility) have destroyed the "erstwhile
quiet communities." There is a social and political edge to *A Shropshire
Lad*, which Housman has contrived to soften by his perfectly rhymed little stanzas which have allowed many readers to consider *only* "universal"
themes like mortality and desire in the abstract. No less than Leavis and
Thompson, however (and no less than Bourne and Sturt), Housman
writes critically of the alienating and destructive conditions of the actual
English lives around him.

XLII. "The Merry Guide"

In trimeter quatrains in alternating rhyme, this poem moves the issues of
time, change, and loss from the social context of the preceding poem
into an allegorical vision. The "merry guide" leads the speaker on a journey from the countryside of azure air and gold waters to travel past the
pastoral landscape (the "solitude of shepherds"), past village life ("ham-

lets"), to a land of devastation ("gardens thinned"): the passage from flourishing beauty to devastation is universalized, "From all the woods that autumn / Bereaves in all the world"; the poem is not about a particular lad's loss of his rural home, but its lyrical intensities rise to sing the sorrows of "the fluttering legion / Of all that ever died." In poems XXXV and XL, the sarcastic juxtapositions occurred within single phrases (as in the juxtaposition of "lovely" with "rotten," and "happy highways" with "lost content"); "The Merry Guide" extends that violent contradiction across the structure of the entire poem (which is one of the longer poems in *A Shropshire Lad*): the "merry" guide is "delightful" in that he displays universal desolation.

More than any other poem by Housman, this lyric of an allegorical journey recalls poems by William Blake, whom Housman was to praise in "The Name and Nature of Poetry" as "the most poetical of all poets"; in that essay, Housman quotes the concluding lyric of Blake's "Gates of Paradise," whose final lines bear comparison with Housman's own beautiful and allegorical lyric: "The Son of Morn in weary Night's decline, / The lost traveller's dream under the hill" (*Prose*, 192). The point is no doctrine or moral meaning—rather, "it is pure and self-existent poetry," Housman says, its emotional power coming not from a moral lesson but from "some region deeper than the mind."

As Housman was to say of Blake's poem, this is a poet's poem: while consciously understood ideas have little to do with its beauty or its emotional force, the hard craft of the poem's making was careful and even laborious: the drafts of the poem in manuscripts in Housman's notebook (where the poem is dated "Sept. 1890") show extensive and meticulous rewriting of the poem (Haber 1966, 206–207).

XLIII. "The Immortal Part"

This poem's 11 quatrains make it (like the immediately preceding poem) one of the longer poems in *A Shropshire Lad*. Its longer lines (four feet each, as opposed to the three feet per line in "The Merry Guide") produce a different music while echoing XXXV, "On the idle hill of summer." The writing and rewriting of this poem, too, were complex, laborious, and long, stretching over several months (Haber 1966, 219).

Cleanth Brooks explains that in this poem "the immortal part of man is his skeleton—not the spirit, not the soul—but the most earthy, the most nearly mineral part of his body."[11] I would add that poem XXXI, "On Wenlock Edge the wood's in trouble," among other poems, had already presented that idea, and that "The Immortal Part" is thus developing a theme that is important in *A Shropshire Lad* as a whole. The first stanza's reference to the repetitive cycles of night and day also develops a theme of meaningless repetition and circularity that has been raised in earlier poems in the volume (including XXXVI).

In form, the poem is almost entirely an imaginary monologue spoken by bones, who affirm that they will last while the temporarily restless life of the body of flesh will not. This imaginary dramatic form is reminiscent of poems like Andrew Marvell's "A Dialogue Between the Soul and Body." The first four lines and the last nine lines are not spoken by the bones, but rather by the person who has heard his bones' meaning: the speaker recognizes the horrible but inescapable truth of the bones's claim that only they (that is, only death) can be permanent; he resolves that "Before this fire of sense decay" he will command the bones to do his will. The *carpe diem* theme of earlier poems (including XXXII) is thus developed here, and this feature of the poem distinguishes it very sharply from Marvell's poems that take the form of the metaphysical dialogue. In Marvell's "A Dialogue Between the Resolved Soul, and Created Pleasure," for example, the opposite happens: the immortal part is the soul (not as in Housman, the material bone), and in Marvell's poem it is the soul that has the last (and moral) word, *refuting* the voice of "Pleasure." Very obviously, Housman adopts the form of imaginary dialogue to deal with the same issues, but from an opposite (and Epicurean) point of view. (As I have suggested earlier, Housman's poems often share the Epicurean ethos of some of Marvell's poems, including "To His Coy Mistress"; in the metaphysical dialogues, however, Marvell voices an opposite sort of doctrine, and in that form, and on that issue, the materialism and atheism of Housman's poetry are directly opposed to the professed faith in an immortal "soul" which is found in Marvell's poems.)

This poem is one of those in which Housman's metrical artistry shows to splendid effect: for example, whereas many of the poem's lines are written in a regular iambic meter (such as line two of the poem, "Or lay me down at night to dream"), some lines use metrical variants skillfully. The second line of stanza five is the only line in that stanza that is not regular iambic; to create a musical slowness which matches its content, the line starts with an accented syllable and ends with two consecutive accents (a spondee), adding emphasis as well as slowing the movement of the line—"Slow the endless night comes on."

Another form of artistry exhibited especially well in this poem is the interweaving of poems by imagery: for example, stanza seven ("Lie down in the bed of dust") recalls poem VII ("Lie down, lie down, young yeoman; / What use to rise and rise?") and poem XVII ("Keeps the bones of man from lying / On the bed of earth"). The image of heat in stanza eight connects the poem with XII ("the heats of hate and lust"); and the image of death as welcome rest in annihilation in stanza eight recalls the similar theme of poem XXVIII, as for example in that poem's final stanza.

XLIV. "Shot? so quick, so clean an ending?"

This is the poem beside which, among his dead brother's papers, Laurence Housman found a newspaper article reporting the suicide of a cadet from Woolwich, who killed himself for shame over his homosexuality and for fear of the disgrace that it might bring. In a way that would appear outrageous, were it not for the quiet and simple language, the first stanza of this poem declares that suicide "was right" in this case: the young man's problem was not to be solved in the social world of late nineteenth-century England; "'Twas best to take it to the grave." Of course the poem's content is *not* outrageous, because it is a harsh attack on the destructive prejudice and unmerited suffering to which many (including persons with homosexual feelings) are condemned. The poem condemns the evil of the affliction, and not the person afflicted.

The use here of the image, "road," is in some ways consistent with the usage of that image in earlier poems: the road leads to the grave. But in another way that image is developed differently here: the brutality (including imprisonment and, for a long historical time, killing) with which homosexual acts had been punished is said to be *worse* than the dust that, by shooting himself in the head, the young man has become. The last stanza's representation of death as a welcome condition of oblivion—"no dreams, no waking"—reaffirms the volume's atheist theme and recalls the feeling of welcome death from earlier poems including XXVIII and XLIII.

XLV. "If it chance your eye offend you"

Coherently with the previous poem, this lyric recommends suicide. In one of the satirical uses of biblical language in *A Shropshire Lad*, the poem begins by echoing the Sermon on the Mount; it is as if, anticipating a religious objection to the previous poem's treatment of suicide and homosexuality, Housman responds by producing a biblical reading on the topic. His first line echoes very directly Matthew 6:29—"if thy right eye offend thee, pluck it out"; and the poem's second (and final) stanza extrapolates: "stand up and end you, / When your sickness is your soul."

XLVI. "Bring, in this timeless grave to throw"

Still coherently with the previous poems, this treatment of death culminates (as does "The Immortal Part") in a direct denial of immortality: from the grave a dead person "never shall arise." Rather than bare doctrinal statement, however, the poem presents imagery that connects it artistically with earlier poems in the collection: "snow" in line two, for example, connects this poem with II, "Loveliest of trees," and with XXXIX, "'Tis time, I think, by Wenlock town." The "timeless grave" is a variation on the theme of "enduring bone" from "The Immortal Part"; the rosemary, the willow, and the buds of springtime also connect this poem with earlier treatments of the finality of death in *A Shropshire Lad*. The awn, "whose flower is blue / A single season, never two," recalls the daffodil in XXIX ("The Lent Lily") which dies on Easter day. The theme of a natural earth that is sympathetic with mortal persons, if only because both are condemned to perish after a meaningless cycle of loss, returns in this poem as well: comfort will be brought to the dead, the speaker imagines, by his companionship with "Whatever will not flower again."

XLVII. "The Carpenter's Son"

The speaker of this poem is (literally) a rustic carpenter who speaks in the idiom of the Shropshire lads; he is to be hanged for an unspecified crime (recalling the hanged man in poem IX), though here the crime is somehow associated with "love" (stanza five). In stanza four, "the people" persecute the condemned man, shaking their fists and cursing at him. The poem is a portrayal of persecution. Though its contemporary topical reference is subtly rather than bluntly made, it is also clear what sort of persecution Housman has in mind. In a poem that Housman never published, he writes of the trial and punishment of Oscar Wilde, for alleged homosexual acts: "they're taking him to prison," Housman's poem says; "they groan and shake their fists"; and as punishment for illegal love, "hanging isn't bad enough" (I quote the poem that Laurence Housman published as poem XVIII among *Additional Poems*). The persecution of the carpenter in poem XLVII, for a crime of love, is obviously analogous.

In England, some homosexual acts (specifically sodomy) were punishable by death from 1533 until 1861. As I have mentioned in an earlier chapter, 80 men were hanged for that reason in the first 30 years of the nineteenth century. Even more were placed in the pillory to be pelted by angry mobs, like the speaker of XLVII, while the police supervised the brutality.

Accordingly, I agree with Leggett that "Housman's poem represents the carpenter's son as regretting his own loss of innocence, for experience has taught him that his efforts to change the nature of man were futile" (Leggett 1970, 23); but the poem's meanings are more concrete, social, and historically specific than what is suggested by Leggett's account of "the burden of the human guilt which comes with knowledge" (Leggett 1970, 25). Critics have recognized for a long time that Housman's adaptation of the figure of Christ to this worldly scene of crime and punishment is audacious in its way; but the depth of the poem's audacity is even more extreme than commentators have been willing or able to explain.

XLVIII. "Be still, my soul, be still; the arms you bear are brittle"

This poem returns to the theme of injustice that is raised in the immediately preceding poem: "here"—that is, in the ordinary social world such as it is—there are "Horror and scorn and hate and fear and indignation"; the speaker's resolution, in response to widespread hatred, is twofold: first, to try not to care ("Let us endure an hour and see injustice done"); and finally to prefer nonexistence: "Oh why did I awake? when shall I sleep again?" Like the poems advocating suicide, and like the earlier poems in the sequence that have treated annihilation (death) as welcome rest, this poem treats the nonexistence before birth (when the matter that became his body was "lightless in the quarry") and the nonexistence after death ("when shall I sleep again?") as preferable to the specifically social torments ("injustice") that are universal. The poem raises skepticism (doubt about whether knowledge is possible): "All thoughts . . . are vain"; one sees "unkindness" but cannot *understand* it—"I muse for why and never find the reason."

The poem's versification is that of the elegiac stanza (iambic pentameter in quatrains of alternating rhyme) except that here each line is elongated to six feet. The musical effect of this drawn-out line is harmonious with the feeling stated in the poem's conclusion, "when shall I sleep again?"

XLIX. "Think no more, lad; laugh, be jolly"

As the previous poem declares that thought is futile, this poem begins by advising a "lad" *not* to think. This poem satirizes its own speaker, whose advice amounts to a recommendation of meaningless and even stupid revelry—"Empty heads and tongues a-talking." The concluding assurance that "'tis only thinking / Lays lads underground" has been belied by many poems earlier in the sequence, which have shown the laying of *everyone* underground, regardless whether (or what) they thought. As the previous poem has said, "high heaven and earth ail from the prime foundation"; if the universe is meaningless matter in random motion, and if the world of human beings is dominated by hatred and injustice, this foolish advice to drink and be merry has a ghastly inadequacy to it which the grim humor of this poem (like poem LXII, below) exposes in satire.[12] I think that Page is mistaken in describing the poem as "advocacy of 'carpe diem'" (Page, 192); instead, the poem positively ridicules a thoughtless and "empty-headed" affectation of such an attitude, in contrast to the poems (XXXII and others) that treat that Horatian theme with high seriousness.

L. *"Clunton and Clunbury"*

This poem artfully belies any simple-minded contrast of countryside (lovely, peaceful, innocent, happy) and city (alienated, unfriendly, filled with struggle and suffering) that sentimental readers might have been tempted to expect. Even in the countryside, and even in youth, "We still had sorrows"; "lads knew trouble"; and likewise in London, an ill-built town, "sorrow is with one still." The "luggage I'd lief set down" (stanza five) recalls the burden that Pilgrim carries on his back in *Pilgrim's Progress*, another fiction of a journey, except that Pilgrim's burden was sin, whereas this speaker's burden consists rather of "griefs," which he carries "on a shoulder / That handselled them long before." (One meaning of "handselled" is "used for the first time.") All of "high heaven and earth ail from the prime foundation" (XLVIII); injustice (and therefore suffering) is universal; and so the sorrow and the trouble are not local, and the reference of the poem is not personal, not specific to a single poet (or persona) but widely generalized across the landscape of country and town.

The poem's final stanza suggests (as other poems have suggested) that the indifference of matter buried in earth (which is what a dead person is) is preferable to the experience of conflict and suffering. The reference to "doomsday" is entirely satirical, because there is no waking to judgment, no afterlife, and in fact no judgment or justice governing the world at all. The organic matter that makes a person is mixed into the organic matter of the soil, and this total annihilation is presented as less painful than life.

LI. "Loitering with a vacant eye"

In another imaginary monologue (like "The Immortal Part"), a young man thinks he hears the speech of an ancient statue, in the Grecian gallery of the British Museum. Through the statue's imagined speech, the theme of alienation in the city is developed here as it was in XLI and L: the statue observes that he is like the young Englishman in that neither of them knew, when they were young, that they would eventually be living among Londoners; the other men in the city are "men whose thoughts are not as mine." As so often in *A Shropshire Lad*, death is represented positively as a laying down of one's burden of suffering (in the second verse paragraph), and the poem concludes brilliantly with a poetic indication of the analogy between this poem about the stone statue that speaks, and "The Immortal Part," where it was the bones who spoke: the final rhyme matches "bone" with "stone."

LII. "Far in a western brookland"

On its surface, this poem (in trimeter quatrains that rhyme in the ballad fashion, *a b c b*) does not seem to add much to the series: by the time we reach the fifty-second poem, we are not surprised to encounter the theme of having come from places "far"—for example, that is the theme of "yon far country" in poem XL. The wanderer hearing the "poplars sigh" is likewise not a surprising image, and the portrayal of the speaker alone and unknown in the city (stanza three) is already familiar from earlier poems, including the immediately preceding poem. Soon, however, the image of the brook (in the first line of this poem) will become important (in poem LIV), and the nocturnal imagery ("windless night-time," "starlit fences") connects this poem with earlier ones: for example, XI, "On your midnight pallet lying," and XXVIII, "The Welsh Marches," and XXX, "Others, I am not the first"; the night is frequently associated with the troubled emergence of primitive desire *and* with the darkness of death. In poem LII, the soul sighing among the glimmering weirs is an image of both.

LIII. "The True Lover"

More clearly than any other poem in the book, this ballad makes obvious the dual meanings of night—desire and death. Like the lad who sighed for longing in poem VI, the lad in this poem who comes here to his lover's door at night asks to be embraced for a moment, because after he departs he will never lie beside another. The meaning is of course clear: naively interpreting its literal reference, we might think that he is going on a journey (perhaps he is a soldier leaving for the foreign war); but as in so many earlier poems, the land to which he travels is a metaphor: as we learn in the penultimate stanza, he has committed suicide, and his "knife has slit / The throat across from ear to ear." The grotesque understatement of the conclusion of that penultimate stanza—the quiet observation that a throat will, under such circumstances, bleed—is perhaps the darkest humor in the book. The satire of both conventional *expectations* of love and of sentimental *poetry* about love could hardly be more stark. In the final stanza, the image of the darkness of night returns, and the boughs (reminiscent of the poplars in the windless night of LII) are "speechless."

LIV. "With rue my heart is laden"

This little poem is perhaps the most memorable—and most beautifully made—in the entire volume. The placement of its poignant beauty beside the dark humor of LIII is an example of the extreme contrasts ("fire and ice") that characterize the poetry of *A Shropshire Lad*. Irony, of course, is a form of extreme contrast, and the nihilistic despair voiced here in terms of pleasant imagery—"golden friends," "rose-lipt maiden," "lightfoot lad"—is another example of a very contrary tone of voice.

   The trimeter quatrains recall poem LII, which is exactly twice as long: the melancholy tone, too, is common to these two poems, and so is the image of the brook: the shortening of the poem is forcefully effective as a formal metaphor in itself of the cutting off of a life, which is the poem's literal subject—boys dead in line six, and girls dead in line seven. The union of the persons with the earth—in a variant of the sympathy-of-nature theme, as in poem XLI—is disturbing because it is death that unifies the persons with the earth, and furthermore the death of everything lovely is precisely the topic of the poem's last line, which presents the natural earth as "fields where roses fade."

LV. "Westward on the high-hilled plains"

The westward direction in this poem's opening line is an echo of the
"western brookland" of poem LII, continuing the fiction of a lad from
the western county, Shropshire, who is now alienated in London. The
second line of the poem returns to the question of the speaker's origins
(as in poem LI, where the statue mentions that the lad was born "far
away"); but the last two lines of the first stanza raise the Lucretian
theme of materialism, wherein the same organic matter is recycled
among different persons over vast historical time. The second stanza,
then, extends the changeless repetition of life in meaningless cycles of
merely temporary activity that had been developed in poem XXXVI:
here, instead of sentimentalized boys enjoying pastoral happiness among
remembered hills of the homeland, the speaker imagines lads who
"Tread the mill I trod before." The image of futility is doubly effective:
not only is their daily round of activity represented as a treadmill (a
device for exerting oneself to go nowhere), but furthermore the lads
mentioned are represented as meaninglessly repeating the same cycles
that the speaker had undergone.

The third stanza then introduces into this poem the theme of the
troubled night of desire, which had been developed earlier in XI,
XXVIII, XXX, and LII. The final stanza affirms very clearly that
thoughts, like the matter of bodies, simply recycle themselves (which
poem XXXI had already suggested in connection with the ancient
Roman); the stanza contains imagery of time (the cycle of night and
morning), and it ends with a bald assertion that (as poem XXVI had
suggested) faithlessness and betrayal are constant among the mortals
trudging along the treadmill of their lives. Like poem L, this poem
makes it clear that *A Shropshire Lad* is not designed to sentimentalize the
loveliness of country as opposed to city: the degradation of meaningless
exertion in short lives of betrayal and uselessness is common in the
crowded city and the western brookland alike.

LVI. "The Day of Battle"

The antiwar theme with which *A Shropshire Lad* began returns here very
clearly, as the second line voices opposition to the military summons
mentioned in line one. What the guns say to the soldier is that he can
flee or be dead forever. The second stanza is the soldier's remark to his
comrade: he would flee if that would save him (there is here no patriotic

dedication to dying for one's country); but as the speaker says in stanza three, to run away is bootless, because he will die as surely on another day; cowards are not mourned when their corpses are taken home, and for that reason—"though the best is bad"—he advises his comrade to "take the bullet in your brain." This is a grisly debunking of the sales pitch of patriotism, as though to fight for one's country were glorious (and that is the sales pitch which is ridiculed in poem III, "The Recruit"): in the point of view represented here, to join the royal cause is simply to "see your slain," and nothing more noble than slaughter is associated with the imperial wars.

Leggett suggests that the poem presents an example of "facing death squarely without flinching" (Leggett 1970, 29), and that form of militaristic propaganda would later prove useful in the opinions of government supporters and even some booksellers. As I mentioned in an earlier chapter, Housman reported with some ridicule that the manager of Kegan Paul, first publisher of *A Shropshire Lad*, "was particularly captivated with the military element; so much so that he wanted me at first to make the whole affair . . . into a romance of enlistment" (*Letters*, 36). But the patriotic propaganda is flatly contradicted by the meanings of the poems, especially those that attack with irony the recruitment, enlistment, and slaughter of youth who die in hypocritically justified wars of imperialistic conquest. In 1915, Walter Raleigh asked for Housman's permission to print some of his poems in a broadsheet for distribution among the soldiers in World War I (*Letters*, 140). Evidently, Raleigh somehow thought that Housman's poetry about war was patriotic or (as Leggett's account might suggest) somehow inspiring. The bitter irony of the antiwar poems is sufficiently skillful to have misled more than one reader of *A Shropshire Lad*.

The poem's tetrameter couplets are the same form of verse that Housman uses in poem XXXVI, which is about the long road of night that bears the wanderer far away in a cyclical route to nowhere. Again, the antiwar theme is assimilated with the more general nihilism that treats human life and the earth as scenes of repetitious futility and suffering.

LVII. "You smile upon your friend to-day"

Nowhere in the collection is the negative theme of meaningless life and final death joined more clearly with the positive theme of Epicurean devotion to what happiness one can find. The "bullet in your brain" which ends LVI is juxtaposed with the wistful but honest recognition voiced carefully in this little poem's ballad stanzas: sympathy and kindness with friend and lover are short and small, and it is *always* late, given the brevity of life; but "I shall have lived a little while / Before I die for ever." In his short story "Death Constant Beyond Love," Gabriel García Márquez alludes to this poem, and his story represents a development of its theme: amidst meaningless propaganda, brutality, and betrayal, Senator Sanchez in García Márquez's story has learned "that he would be dead forever by next Christmas";[13] as in the grim humor of Housman's poem LIII ("The True Lover"), Sanchez seeks a moment of love as if that would somehow redeem him from the degradation of death, but the falsehoods and betrayals that fill the characters' lives render that conventional fantasy meaningless.

LVIII. "When I came last to Ludlow"

Like poems LII and LIV, this poem uses trimeter quatrains; like poem XXXVI it uses a repeated line about the moon; and it is similar to those poems in other ways as well. Like XXXVI it is about circular movements and their eventual returns; and it recalls from LIV the lament for the loss of those who were one's friends (the death of lads and maidens in LIV; here one death and one long imprisonment that removes "Ned"). The return of lines one and two as lines seven and eight is itself an enactment of the return (to Ludlow) which the poem is about; and the tone of sadness, loss, and regret that ends the poem is an enactment of the change from former gladness to present loss which forms the little narrative's content.

LIX. "The Isle of Portland"

This poem's three ballad-stanzas use an added rhyme for the first and third lines in each stanza. These verses are thus formally the same as the stanzas of many previous poems in *A Shropshire Lad*, all of which are about time, change, loss, and (usually) death: poems I, IX, XVI, XVIII, XX, XXII, XXV, XXXVI, XXXVIII, XXXIX, XL, LIII, and LVII. As practicing poets know well, this coincidence of a particular verse form with a particular theme or set of emotions is not necessarily contrived deliberately, and, for that matter, many poems in *A Shropshire Lad* develop those themes and feelings with other verse forms; but the musical echo imparted by the prosody is likely to bring about *other* associations among the poems, including thematic associations, whether by conscious design or otherwise. Death of soldiers in foreign wars, death by hanging, suicide, death as the absurd but unavoidable and absolute end of every human life—these topics of the poems, associated by the common verse form and orchestrated throughout the book as a whole, provide a more richly woven texture of meanings and feelings than simply the sum of individual poems. Each poem in the cluster gathers intellectual associations and emotional resonance from the others, and Housman's careful versification is both a sign of this subtle form of unity and a musical means for its achievement.

In "The Isle of Portland," Housman begins by alluding to "Dover Beach" by Matthew Arnold, one of his favorites since his undergraduate years at Oxford: like Arnold's poem, "The Isle of Portland" begins with a speaker looking at the sea (the Straits of Dover) separating France from England; the water at night is illuminated (by the moon in "Dover Beach" and by starlight in "The Isle of Portland"). The nostalgia in Arnold's poem is focussed on lost faith (Christianity having become obsolete), and in Housman's poem, it is focussed on a lost (dead) friend; the contrasting imagery of lights and darks is common to the two poems; and whereas Arnold's poem represents modern civilization in the metaphor of armies of ignorant men destroying each other meaninglessly in the dark, Housman produces the metaphorical (and also quite literal) example of an island on which convicted criminals have quarried stones, amidst which lies the corpse of a person who was once the speaker's friend.

The final stanza of "The Isle of Portland" echoes the seventh stanza of poem XLIII, "The Immortal Part": both contain the imperative ("Lie down in the bed of dust" in XLIII; here, "Lie you easy"); but whereas "The Isle of Portland" contains the good wish that the oblivion of death may be preferable to the pain of life ("luckier may you find the night / Than ever you found the day"), in "The Immortal Part," that wish is denied in advance: "morn is all the same as night."

LX. "Now hollow fires burn out to black"

In one of the most beautifully compressed poems in *A Shropshire Lad* (a book distinguished by beautiful compression), Housman begins by continuing the imagistic theme of opposed darks and lights: the "hollow fires" that "burn out" are a literal and visible fact in the story of a soldier about to depart in the morning; they are also a disturbing metaphor for a human life. The conventional (not to say, inhumanly mechanical) movement of squaring one's shoulders to march is likewise a literal element in the story of the departing soldier, while it is also a portrayal of foolish optimism, at best, and (worse) it is a suggestion of mindless and brain-washed conformity, produced by the propaganda of the war industry.

The word "nought" in stanza two is an excellent example of one sort of richly contradictory meaning that Housman's irony can achieve: literally, the line says that there is nothing to fear; but the concept of nothingness becomes both frightening and profound, in a modernist way, in the poem's brilliantly framed conclusion: "In all the endless road you tread / There's nothing but the night"—the nihilism is total. The road is a familiar metaphor in this collection for the journey of the soldier, the progress of a human life, and the meaningless processes of human history, a circuitous path to nowhere.

Not only is this very short poem composed to develop a richness of meaning internally: it also orchestrates themes from the collection as a whole. In "Reveille," the waking of soldiers is represented in a summons to rise and move onward, though it is only a dark and unknown grave to which the soldiers move. The last stanza of that poem, too, moves beyond the particular reference to consider human beings as a merely temporary mixture of clay and blood. In poem XXII, a soldier being sent off to a foreign war becomes a metaphor for the universal condition of mortal human beings. In poem XXII, the social *and* metaphysical problem of alienation is represented in the symbolism of a soldier at whom the speaker looks for a moment in mutual ignorance of any thoughts that they might have: the world is a vast wasteland populated by strangers at painful distance from one another. In poem XXIII, the image of the road is used again as the men depart, never to return: there, as here, the threefold meanings include the literal road down which the young men go, the journeying of soldiers to their distant military destination, and the linear progress of all persons to their graves. In XXXIV ("The New Mistress"), the line of soldiers "wears thinner and the dropping dead lie thick." In XXXV, "The roads of earth" are, literally, the routes of soldiers who march off, "all to die"; but the phrase ("of earth") generalizes the meaning, as here in poem LX the meaning is generalized by the phrase "all the endless road you tread." Poems XXXV and LX both represent the futile movement of all humanity toward the meaningless inertness of buried bones.

LXI. "Hughley Steeple"

This poem's eight-line stanzas are almost identical in form with those of poem XIII, "When I was one-and-twenty": all of the lines are three metrical feet in length, and the rhyme scheme divides the eight-line

stanza into two sets of four. In XIII, however, the use of "feminine" endings links the odd-numbered lines, whereas the even-numbered lines are
linked by rhyme; here, *both* rhyme and the use of "feminine" endings
link the odd-numbered lines.

In the first stanza the speaker refers (like the speaker of "The Isle of
Portland") to the graves of dead friends: the steeple tower that literally
divides shade from sun works metaphorically like the dark and the light
in "The Isle of Portland" and, in poem LXI, depicts the severance of the
living from the dead, as the second stanza states quite explicitly: "The
dead are more in muster / At Hughley than the quick." The use of the
military term *muster* links the poem to the preceding lyric and likewise to
the many other poems in *A Shropshire Lad* that treat military death literally, while here the usage is entirely metaphorical. The second stanza
indicates that at the south of the church the ordinary dead are buried,
whereas suicides are buried in the churchyard south of the building. And
the final stanza suggests that north and south, ordinary death and suicide, are not after all significant distinctions: "'tis only / A choice of
friends one knows." Grimly the speaker concludes the poem by suggesting that whether he kills himself or dies normally, he will in either case
be joining a large number of others. Buried in the soil of earth—in fact,
being soil in earth—the dead are not different from one another.

LXII. "Terence, this is stupid stuff"

As Housman had considered entitling this book *Poems of Terence Hearsay*,
it is clear that the "Terence" of this poem's title is the character imagined
speaking some or all of the poems; hence, this poem is metapoetry, a
poem about the preceding poems in particular and about poetry in general. Like poem XLIX ("Think no more, lad; laugh, be jolly"), this poem
is satirical: XLIX satirizes its first speaker, whose advice amounts to a
recommendation of meaningless and even stupid revelry—"Empty heads
and tongues a-talking." In XLIX, if the world is a place of meaningless
motion, whose inhabitants are thoughtless perpetrators of hatred and
injustice, this foolish advice to drink and be merry is exposed as a brutal-
ly inadequate—even beastly and stupid—response. That response is represented here, in "Terence, this is stupid stuff," by the *other* character who
speaks first, saying to "Terence" that eating and drinking and dancing
are desirable whereas his poetry, which is "melancholy," is not. The
remainder of the poem is Terence's reply.

Terence indicates that beer and ale are more effective than poetry at
temporarily amusing those who are unwilling or unable "to think": if

one would like what is called entertainment (to use a twentieth-century expression), then (Terence recommends) one can drink ale. If (to state the point another way) one prefers falsehood to truth, "Look into the pewter pot [that is, drink beer] / To see the world as the world's not." The second verse paragraph indicates that there are many persons and business enterprises who will gladly sell commodities of delusion for people who dislike the truth. However, Terence observes, there is a problem with enjoyable illusions of happiness: "The mischief is that 'twill not last." Terence says that he has travelled for enjoyment to the fair, become drunk, and enjoyed the illusion that all was well and that he was himself "a sterling lad"; drunk, he slept "in lovely muck," to discover when he awoke that "the tale was all a lie; / The world, it was the old world yet." Induced by alcohol, drugs, advertisements, or popular entertainments, a lovely falsification of the world is produced by imagery that is *not* true to "the way of things" (to use Lucretius's metaphor, *De rerum natura*). The stupid, the thoughtless, and the gullible buy such falsifications (as they buy beer, advertised commodities, and popular entertainments); Terence does not buy them.

This is Terence's short account of "the way of things": "Luck's a chance, but trouble's sure." Terence does not want to deny or ignore this fact about the world in which he lives. He wants to think about it, to "face it as a wise man would." To do so, Terence says, will be better preparation for adversity, enabling him to "train for ill and not for good," because the world has, in fact, "much less good than ill." Representing his poetry under the metaphor of a beverage, he says that, if its flavor is sour, "The better for the embittered hour." He does not produce poems that confront the pain and sorrow of life for the purpose of disturbing others, but rather to help them in connection with the sorts of experience that will dominate (and terminate) their lives: "I will friend you, if I may, / In the dark and cloudy day."

The poem's last verse paragraph tells a parable: an ancient king, Mithridates, had a custom of eating poisoned meat and poisoned drink as a preparation for thought; his subjects looked on in fear when he took these poisoned items, but it was they who were harmed: he had made himself immune to the poison precisely by taking doses of it.

Of course Housman knew that multitudes of people had always bought stories with happy endings more gladly than they would buy melancholy reflections on the pain and losses of mortal life such as it is. People prefer the illusion of hope to the truth of defeat and despair; people prefer lies about how life is meaningful to the bitter truth that life is momentary pleasure or pain and then permanent annihilation. The ancient skeptical philosophers (and many philosophers since) have pointed out that people are more likely to believe what they prefer than to believe what is true.[14] In "Terence, this is stupid stuff," Housman is in part defending his poetic volume against the predictable objection that his poems present painful truths that many persons would rather ignore or deny by means of superstition, alcohol, or artificially happy stories, which commercial firms sell for profit to a public that will pay good money to be cheered up. The concluding parable suggests that one is better prepared for the destructive elements of life and the world if one has thought of them from time to time, rather than drunkenly falling into delusions.

Leggett has suggested that Housman's defense of his pessimistic poetry has something in common with psychoanalytic theories, and specifically Sigmund Freud's essay "Beyond the Pleasure Principle," and with a tradition of thought about art associated with Aristotle's theory of catharsis: the suggestion is that, paradoxically, people sometimes take pleasure in confrontation with their fears, or at least experience a fascination with their own deepest fears and pain. Leggett rejects the pleasure principle as a justification of poetry in Housman's view: he argues that "the imagery and structure of 'Terence' serve to deny two of the most widely held beliefs about poetry—that its function is to provide pleasure and that it does not require us to interact with the real world" (Leggett 1978, 133). The concept of entertainment and the concept of enjoyment may be shallow, false, inadequate, and unworthy for a good life, in comparison with things like wisdom and human sympathy (see the third verse paragraph) and endurance (the theme of the parable of Mithridates).

It may be this set of concepts, suggested by poems including "Terence, this is stupid stuff," which led so many reviewers and critics to describe Housman's thought as "stoical."[15] Epictetus, the great moralist among ancient philosophers, advised his followers in this way: "Let death and exile and everything that is terrible appear before your eyes every day, especially death; and you will never have anything contemptible in your thoughts or crave anything excessively."[16] While the poet in "Terence, this is stupid stuff" clearly voices a related set of attitudes, there is no need or reason to conclude that Housman (the person) *was* a Stoic; there is more (and more persuasive) evidence that he approved Epicurean thought, as I have indicated in an earlier chapter of the present book. Epicureans ancient and modern also argue that the end of life in natural death should be kept in view, intensifying the devotion to beauty and love, which in the way of things are transitory. Among writers in Housman's lifetime, Pater developed this point of view, in connection with art, most memorably and influentially in the conclusion to *The Renaissance*. But, in Housman's poem, "Terence" is a fictitious character, no less than the uneducated drunk who upbraids him within the poem and who prefers bestial satisfactions to what the poet represents as wisdom.

The apparent Epicureanism in *A Shropshire Lad* led some early reviewers and critics to compare Housman's book with Edward Fitzgerald's *The Rubaiyat of Omar Khayyam* (see for example Holbrook Jackson's 1919 essay on Housman, reproduced in Gardner, 102–109). Harold Munro wrote in 1920 that "some one has called *A Shropshire Lad* the "English Rubaiyat"—a suggestive comparison. These English lyrics present a western version of that philosophy of life contained in Fitzgerald's beautiful fragment from the Eastern poet. Neither work is pessimistic: each offers a compensation for the certainty that death is a final end to personal existence. The western compensation is Friendship."[17] Jackson's discussion of "Terence, this is stupid stuff" identifies the issue of the poem's apparent pessimism in terms that are consistent with Housman's own metapoetry here: "People are frightened of the word pessimism, and the word optimism has become a folly and a weariness of the flesh. Nowadays it is tripped about the market-place like a vain thing, so that wise folk shun it. But one should beware of labels whatever they are. . . . Housman must be ranked amongst the happy poets because he is strong enough to look sorrow in the face" (Gardner, 108). Of course Housman was aware, as important poets of the past couple of centuries have consistently been aware, that people fear pessimism and prefer advertisements for happy living through the market place; they prefer (in the symbolism of Housman's poem) beer drinking to thinking. Bottoms up.

LXIII. "I hoed and trenched and weeded"

The concluding poem in *A Shropshire Lad* is also metapoetry: as Benjamin Gilbert Brooks pointed out in 1940, this poem is a "justification of his method." The first stanza indicates that the product of the speaker's labor (literally, flowers; metaphorically, poems) were not admired because they were not in fashion; the critical implication is that temporary fashions in art, ratified only by convention, determine the reception of the work. In the second stanza the speaker indicates that he scatters the seeds of flowers for others (lads like him) to find when he lies "below them, / A dead man out of mind." The third stanza is a compressed retelling of the parable of the sower, from Matthew 13:

> Behold, a sower went forth to sow: And when he sowed, some seeds fell by the way side, and the fowls came and devoured them up: Some fell upon stony places, where they had not much earth: and forthwith they sprung up, because they had no deepness of earth: And when the sun was up, they were scorched; and because they had no root, they withered away. And some fell among thorns; and the thorns sprung up, and choked them: But other fell into good ground, and brought forth fruit, and some an hundredfold, some sixtyfold, some thirtyfold. Who hath ears to hear, let him hear.

In Housman's version of the parable in stanza three, some of the seed that the gardener scattered was devoured by birds, and some marred by seasons; some, however, grew to flower (and they are like "solitary stars," recalling the image of stars from "The Isle of Portland"). The fourth (and last) stanza of the poem is a final example of the painful irony that Housman has used so often in *A Shropshire Lad*: while (positively) these starlike flowers will bloom every year "As light-leaved spring comes on," to be worn as ornaments by lads like himself, the stanza contradicts the apparent tone of gladness: the lads who do this will be "luckless," and it will happen "When I am dead and gone." With something of the melancholy tone that is sounded by many of the poems in the collection, but also with some wit, the last word in the book is the "gone" of "dead and gone."

Chapter Five

Last Poems, More Poems, Additional Poems

Last Poems

In October 1922 *Last Poems* appeared to considerable acclaim. For example, on the day of its publication, a favorable review appeared in the *Times*. The publisher of the book, Grant Richards, had arranged for an initial printing of 4,000 copies, but these had all been sold in advance, and several additional printings were required to meet the demand. Within a year, as Page reports, 21,000 copies had been printed (Page, 132). Reviewers found *Last Poems* to be similar to *A Shropshire Lad* in a variety of ways—in "outlook," in "theme," in the poems' "modern paganism," and in their "poignant tone of realistic stoicism." Edmund Gosse found a "completer technical excellence" in *Last Poems*, in comparison with *A Shropshire Lad*, and one reviewer ("D.C.T." in the *Cambridge Review*) found the poems in the later book "more thoughtful, more hopeless, more mature."[1]

R. W. Postgate wrote of the "marvelous perfection" of *Last Poems*, but found behind its artistry a "dead soul": Postgate suggested that Housman perceived the failure of all efforts to ameliorate modern evils—and specifically evils caused by the "industrial machine" of modern civilization. Postgate suggests that there is some escapism in Housman's devotion of himself to the laborious task of meticulous scholarship on the obscure ancient poet Manilius, in whom no one was interested (see Gardner, 27).

Postgate's observations help to situate Housman's poems in their historical time and place. While some of the 41 poems in *Last Poems* were written much earlier (the earliest that can be dated with confidence were written in 1895),[2] at least 12 of the poems were written or finished in the year in which the book appeared, and the careful assembly of the poems into a thematically coherent book—a book that is to be understood as a poetic unit in itself—was also performed in 1922. Like *A Shropshire Lad, Last Poems* is a product of its time.

The most obviously relevant historical events that intervened between *A Shropshire Lad* and *Last Poems* were imperial wars, chiefly the Boer War and World War I. In an earlier chapter I have indicated briefly how Housman's life and thought were affected by those wars; the poems in *Last Poems* take their meanings in whole or in part in the context of global bloodshed, economic exploitation, personal and cultural devastation, and manipulative state apparatuses that promoted those imperial efforts.

Before World War I began, as Kenneth O. Morgan has written, there was a "prospect of nation-wide industrial paralysis"; there was "a state of near civil war in Ireland"; there was ethnic violence in the Balkans, which came to a crisis when Archduke Ferdinand of Austria was killed in Bosnia (at Sarajevo) in June 1914. That assassination led immediately to the outbreak of World War I. In England, conscription was begun in May 1916; there was "manipulation of the news services"; there was "censorship of the press"; there were "government-sponsored legends" to promote the war with propaganda. Antiwar activists were persecuted, including colleagues of Housman at Cambridge, as I have already shown. The reality of this censorship and suppression is important for the interpretation of Housman's writings, as I shall be showing below.

The horror of the war was extreme: in one military episode alone (the British attack on the Somme), there were 420,000 casualties, including 60,000 on one day. Altogether in the war, 3,250,000 men were killed or wounded: "half an entire generation of young men" were "wiped out." At home in England, the industrial machine and the machine of state power were massively and permanently increased. Morgan reminds us that the war "was, in all senses, a profoundly imperial war, fought for empire as well as for king and country"; one symbol of imperial power was the rebuilding of Delhi in India by British architects, such that the city was "dominated by a massive Viceroy's residence and Secretariat buildings" (Morgan, 582–93).

The first eight poems in *Last Poems* are about soldiers: in poem I ("The West"), the soldier is presented in the context of the journey, in imagery familiar from *A Shropshire Lad*: the sending of the soldier to a foreign war is at once a literal story and a metaphorical representation of a vision of human life as a temporary motion on a material earth, a motion that ends utterly at physical death. Poem I ("The West") is about both the soldier on the road and philosophical materialism; poem VII places the soldier on the road in the context of May as a season of momentary beauty. Poem XVIII develops the idea of metaphysical nothingness ("nought") in the metaphor of the road. Poem XXXI ("Hell Gate") ridicules superstition, referring to the "hell within" rather than the supposed hell of religious superstition, and this poem begins, "Onward on the road again." Epicureanism like that which is voiced in many poems in *A Shropshire Lad* appears in poem IX, with its May flowers and its representation of life as a naturalistic recycling of elements—"The flesh will grieve on other bones than ours"; and the fourth stanza uses the metaphor of the road to produce what is perhaps the most memorable statement of Housman's Epicureanism in verse:

> It is in truth iniquity on high
> > To cheat our sentenced souls of aught they crave,
> And mar the merriment as you and I
> > Fare on our long fool's-errand to the grave.

As this poem (and others like it) make clear, the imperial wars in which millions of young men are slaughtered and maimed are one example of an historically larger problem—an ancient problem—which is the meaningless recycling of flesh and bone, moved here and there by the temporary winds of thought and feeling, but arriving finally nowhere, like the dark earth in its countless (and pointless) revolutions in empty space. This ancient problem, this condition of meaningless motion in an empty universe, has always afflicted humanity, and it always will: "The troubles of our proud and angry dust / Are from eternity, and shall not fail" (IX).

The imagery of cycles (cycles of life, cycles of the seasons) returns in many poems in *Last Poems*: in XVI ("Spring Morning"), April renews flowers under one's feet, and human hope also flowers in the early season; there follow winter, pain, scorn, and a death wish, and the poem concludes (like poems XXV, XXVI, and XXVII in *A Shropshire Lad*) with a short story of faithlessness. Poem XIX is a poem on the subjects of superstitions, in which the rotation of days and nights is paralleled with the rotation of the living and the dead, while illusions and dreams temporarily torment the speaker of the poem. In poem XX, the metaphors of rotation are numerous and they are presented with special artfulness: nightfall, the fall of winter, the cycle of life and death, and "the turning globe" are imagistic repetitions of the theme of cyclicality; and the poem's versification is contrived to represent rotation, too, as each stanza consists of two tercets (that is, two units of three lines each) which do not rhyme internally, but which rhyme with each other; the rhyme sounds rotate in units of three, mimicking the imagery of rotation which the poem produces as a metaphor for the recycling of matter (in motion) which is the ancient story of the earth.

The Epicurean idea that thoughts and feelings are recycled material energies, no less than physical matter such as human bodies, was of course developed in *A Shropshire Lad*, in poems including XXXI ("On Wenlock Edge"). This idea returns in *Last Poems*, as in XXXIV ("The First of May"): the speaker thinks of Ludlow in the spring, in his youth; now, new people walk between the flowering trees which the speaker remembers, and "Our thoughts, a long while after, / They think, our words they say." The cosmic scale of these meaningless cycles of repetition is nowhere more clear than in poem XXXVI ("Revolution"): the rotation of the round earth on its axis and the movement of night around the planet (on "wheels of darkness") are followed, in the poem, by the mounting of the sun to noon; but then instantly it "Has crossed the nadir," and "the subterranean dark," in its eternal round movement, "begins to climb." The poem's meaning is only superficially astronomical; the planetary examples of darkness revolving over spaces where sunlight had been are metaphors of natural and human cycles that are treated variously but concisely in poem after poem: hope and fear, birth and death, love and betrayal, joy and desolation, the desire of glory and the disillusionment of luckless men reduced to despair.

In poem II, the resigned speaker thinks of the "golden" young men who have died all over the world; he thinks not only of current events but of "old ill fortunes"; aware of the futility, he nonetheless straps on his "sword that will not save." That mood establishes an emotional context for the next poem in the collection (III, "Her strong enchantments failing"), which is one of the most extraordinary poems that Housman ever published: in contrast to poems that treat directly Queen Victoria and the soldiers whom she calls to service (including poem V), poem III presents itself in symbolic or allegorical guise, as if it were about "The Queen of air and darkness" in some mythological sense, rather than the Queen of England; after two poems about the death of soldiers in foreign wars, the speaker of the poem imagines killing the Queen; Housman's reasons for using the veiled and ostensibly mythological vocabulary are obvious.

This poem also illustrates an important fact about the structure and composition of *Last Poems*: the poem had been published before, under the title of "The Conflict," in a magazine produced at King Edward's School in Bath; it had also been included in the first set of printed proofs for *A Shropshire Lad*, but then Housman deleted it before that volume was printed (Page, 197; Bayley, 163–64). Then in 1922, Housman published the poem again, placing it between a poem about "fighting" and a poem about a dead soldier (IV, "Illic Jacet"), which is followed by a poem that begins "The Queen she sent to look for me."

There is further political satire (though subtle enough to avoid official animosity or retribution): some of the political themes associate the machinery of state power with the machinery of religious institutions and the superstitions which they promulgate: for example, poem XII repudiates both "The laws of God" and "the laws of man"; poem XXVIII is about "the poor"; XXXI ("Hell Gate") ridicules the old superstition about eternal punishment and attacks the political tyranny that that superstition had been used, historically, to support. Poem VI ("Lancer") is a monologue which voices an implicit critique of British imperialism, and which rises from that topical reference to treat (as many poems in *A Shropshire Lad* had done) the concept of death as rest and respite from the pain and struggle of a brutalizing life of conflict. The notion of death as a welcome rest appears again in VIII and XXIX, and in both cases it arises in connection with soldiers, whose death amidst exploitation and delusion becomes a metaphor for futile lives in general.

Poem XXXVII ("Epitaph on an Army of Mercenaries") uses a subtle form of mockery. It was first published during World War I (in the *Times*, October 1917), and the poem includes parody of the rhetoric of patriotic propaganda. British military trouble is represented absurdly as "the day when heaven was falling"; those who "saved" British interests (which are hyperbolically called "the sum of things") did not do so for patriotic purposes, but "for pay." Ghussan R. Greene has justly observed that "the implications of this poem make it hard to understand why it was not omitted from *The Selected Poems of A. E. Housman*, 'the first of the Armed Services Editions printed for free distribution overseas to American servicemen in the Second World War.'"[3]

As in the "Epitaph on an Army of Mercenaries," the theme of illusion frequently appears in connection with deliberately propagated deceptions with political purposes. In XXI the imagery of "fairies" and their "dances" is undercut by the mention of India, where British imperialism had (very obviously) taken both military and commercial forms; the poem's speaker passes in thought from "fairies" to India, and then "won-

ders what's to pay." The speaker in XXXII remembers that, when he
was younger, he entertained many illusions; he would "nurse resolves
and fancies." In contrast to these pleasant expectations, the poem concludes with soldiers being sent across the ocean to die in foreign wars.
Poem XXXIII begins in a scene of dark nature, represented as "the roar-
ing wood of dreams"; the second stanza presents the imagination of a
tormented person to whom there come "From deep clay, from desert
rock, / From the sunk sands of the main," the memories (like ghosts) of
those who never returned his love; he then thinks of the dead, who must
lie down now "In gross marl" (that is, in crumbling soil) in foreign lands.

Perhaps most beautifully and poignantly, poem XL represents the
joy of the young in nature as a "tune the enchantress plays" in "soft
September" or "under blanching mays"; and "marshalled under moons
of harvest / Stand still all night the sheaves"; in winter, beeches "stain
the wind with leaves." This natural beauty is surrendered, now, to others: "Possess, as I possessed a season, / The countries I resign," where
the road "Would mount the hill and shine." The brightness of the
beautiful promise of youth is, finally, illusion, as is clear to the dispos-
sessed and the dying: "For nature, heartless, witless nature, / Will neither care nor know."

The idea that lies that comfort people are frequently preferred to
truths that are bitter is developed explicitly in XXV, "The Oracles,"
which begins by saying clearly enough that, in contrast to a demystified
and modern world, the past of our civilization was given to superstition:
believers in fictitious deities would consult oracles and take the sound of
the wind for messages from gods; in this way the "gods told lies of old."
As in the symbolic terms of "Hell Gate," Housman replaces the false
belief in an external God or gods with a recognition of the entirely natural and human source of meaning—"The heart within, that tells the
truth." When it is the actual human heart that is the "cave of oracles,"
this is what the priestess says: "That she and I should surely die and
never live again."

The brilliantly compressed ending of "The Oracles" moves the
poem's themes from the merely general reflection on human mortality
to engage more closely the antiwar theme and the moral idea (of
Epicureanism) that is consistent in Housman's work. The poem uses a
classical allusion to refer at once to the horrible human cost of imperial
war *and* to Housman's Epicurean theme of seizing what beauty one can
in the momentary interval of life: the poem's last stanza refers to the

ancient war in which the Persian armies marched to attack the hopeless-
ly outnumbered Spartans, who were certain to "die for nought"; knowing that their futile deaths were to come on the morrow, "The Spartans
on the sea-wet rock sat down and combed their hair."

Just as *A Shropshire Lad* ends with metapoetry, with poem LXIII representing Housman's poems under the metaphor of flowers and their
seeds that will blossom into temporary life and color for others "When I
am dead and gone," so too *Last Poems* ends with a poem about poetry.
Poem XLI, "Fancy's Knell," is about two deaths: the death of the poet
(as in *A Shropshire Lad* LXIII), but also the death of imagination. In the
metaphor of a country lad playing his flute for dances, after the labor of
the day had ended, Housman represents his poetry pessimistically—"idle
pleasures"—while over all England "Advanced the lofty shade." That
image of the advancing darkness refers literally to the night that followed an evening of flute music and dancing, but it refers metaphorically to the moral darkness and despair of a civilization. In the final stanza,
the impending death of the flautist (the poet) is the literal reference of
the imagery of dispersal: Housman ends his *Last Poems* with a painfully
brief acknowledgment of the dissolution into nothingness of his art and
himself: "To air the ditty, / And to earth I."

More Poems and *Additional Poems*

Housman's will, which is dated 1832, gave to Laurence Housman permission to gather from his notebooks those poems which seemed to be
finished and which seemed to be as good as the average of what he had
published himself. After Housman's death in 1936, Laurence followed
these instructions, producing the book entitled *More Poems*. Some of
these poems were written early: for example, LXVIII, "Parta Quies,"
which ends the volume by representing death as a welcome relief from
conflict and suffering, was first published in 1881, in a magazine at
Oxford; and that theme had been recurrent in Housman's poetry from
his first collection onward, as I have shown in earlier chapters of this
book. Poems X through XXX belong to the set of *Terence* poems from
which Housman had assembled *A Shropshire Lad* in 1896.[4]

More Poems is a beautifully organized collection, but this time the aesthetic achievement of producing a poetically coherent volume is Laurence's
work rather than A. E. Housman's. The poems are not arranged chrono-
logically (and this fact is obvious, because the last poem in the collection

had been published separately in 1881), nor by topic, but rather artistically. The scholar who has argued most extensively for the coherence and
excellence of *More Poems* summarizes the unity of the book in this way:

> Three strategies unify the volume that Laurence assembled from his
> brother's verse manuscripts: first, patterns of imagistic and thematic
> development orchestrate the poetic structure of the book, even as each
> poem embodies such a poetic structure. Second, an estrangement of asser-
> tion characterizes the statements presented in the poems, whereby irony,
> contradiction, and unresolved paradox take the place of dogmatic state-
> ments that might be taken for truth. And, finally, an ethos of sympathy
> provides a moral and emotional tone that unifies the poems, and, more
> largely, the book. Analysis of *any* of the forty-nine poems in the volume
> will disclose these principles at work, and comparison of the poems with
> one another will do the same.[5]

For example, in XXXVIII those who have died see only "night for ever";
in XLV the speaker wonders, "What shall I build or write / Against the
fall of night?"; and the volume closes with a poem that begins, "Good
night" (XLVIII). Night and death are first feared (as in XLV) and then
finally welcomed as "imperishable peace" (XLVIII): that phrase's wonderful irony is the observation that (in contrast to myths about immortality) only annihilation is "imperishable." In poem XXV the speaker
departs "into death away, / Not to be born again." Poem III refers in its
first stanza to "the nations of the nadir"—literally foreign countries; in
stanza five, the language has shifted to "the perished nation"; poem XIV
refers to "the perished people"; and XX observes, "The put-to-death, the
perished nation / How sound they sleep!" Again, XLVIII completes the
orchestration of this theme: "Sleep on, sleep sound."

    What has been called the "estrangement of assertion" also appears
within single poems, and likewise it appears as a pattern among different poems in the collection. Poem I ("Easter Hymn") declares no belief
whatsoever, saying only "If" and "But if": the poem leaves its opposed
beliefs in unresolved contradiction. The poem that Laurence Housman
placed next in the collection, "When Israel out of Egypt came," echoes
"The Oracles" (poem XXV in *Last Poems*): the cloudy flame and thunder
of the Israelites' religious myths are now dumb; "To me they have not
come"; the poem's fifth stanza denies that any one will ever (really) go to
the "promised land" of religious fictions; and, in contrast to the wish-ful-
fillment fantasy of eternal life, the poem concludes:

> . . . I will go where they are hid
> That never were begot,
> To my inheritance amid
> The nation that is not.

The poem denies outright the myths that it invokes.

Poem IV, "The Sage to the Young Man," contrasts the viewpoints named in its title and develops the theme of utter nothingness after death, as the sage tells the young man that (in contrast to popular delusions about eternal life) he is not immortal: "Thou wast not born for aye." That line appears again in the next poem in the series, "Diffugere Nives," which is Housman's translation of an ode from Horace (*Odes* 4.7): "The swift hour and the brief prime of the year / Say to the soul, *Thou wast not born for aye*." In both poems, that assertion is estranged—it is never the poet (Housman) who says it, but rather it is spoken by a fictitious character called "the Sage" in poem III, and it is spoken (by personification) by the hour and the season, in a poem by an ancient Latin poet. Furthermore, this poem of pagan myth follows poems on Christian myth ("Easter Hymn") and Hebrew myth ("When Israel out of Egypt came"): by juxtaposing contradictory myths, the poems estrange them all. The falsehood of these myths is involved directly in their historicity: faiths are temporary; they come and go; "Stone, steel, dominions pass, / Faith too, no wonder" (XXIV).

The first stanza in poem XII says that "All things may end"; "truth" is "mortal"; it is relative and temporary. Stanza two, in contradiction, makes statements about what will "last" and what is "Eternal." Inside the one poem, two sets of assertions thereby contradict one another; neither represents a statement of belief. The beliefs nullify each other until, finally, death nullifies them all.

Poem XXXVI is only four lines in length, and it is an imaginary epitaph suitable for a tombstone over dead soldiers. The poem ends with deceptive simplicity and genuine complexity, because it simultaneously states a belief, denies the belief, and voices the painful feeling of that contradiction: "Life, to be sure, is nothing much to lose; / But young men think it is, and we were young."

Poems VI, VII, and VIII present an analogous pattern inside each poem and also among the poems in the series. Inside each poem, contradictory stanzas represent a dialectic of endurance and loss, of death and

survival (see Hoagwood 1986, 84); the consolation of stars (in VI) is succeeded by the loss and annihilation associated with the starless sea (VIII).

The poems from the *Terence* series exhibit another method for achiev-
ing the "estrangement of assertion": the poet (in writing) and Laurence
Housman (in assembling the collection) present conflicting moods, and
not an actually enduring attitude of the author at all. As Laurence says
in his preface to the collection, these poems in the *Terence* series "express,
sometimes contradictorily, the turbulent and changing moods of troubled youth" (p. vii).

Contradiction and dialectical opposition are important in other ways
in the collection as well. Poem XXXV tells the story of Lot's wife,
emphasizing a conflict of unresolved opposites: "Half-way, for one com-
mandment broken, / The woman made her endless halt." The paradox of
"endless halt" is palpable—"endless" denoting an ongoing action in contrast to the "halt." "Half-way" immobilizes the woman, who is neither
here nor there but frozen in uncompleted transit; and the second half of
the poem is not about Lot's wife at all, but rather Lot himself, who did
not halt but who (in entire contrast) "Pursued his road."

Housman's critique of British imperial wars emerges in *More Poems* as
well as his earlier volumes, sometimes in company with his critique of
myth; for example, his poem speaks ostensibly about the illusion of
immortality when he writes, "The realm I look upon and die / Another
man will own" (II). The killing of a soldier by an enemy soldier is narrat-
ed in XXXVII as a chilling instance of murderous nonsense in which the
impulse to sympathy and friendship are pointlessly cancelled in the brutality of the killing. Poem XXXIX is about "blood and smoke and shot,"
and about a soldier who ran away from the fight and who lived, in contrast to his brave comrades who are dead and buried in "a field afar." In
XL a soldier is said to be "cheap to the King." The "nations of the nadir"
in poem III are the countries of southern Africa where British men
(including Housman's brother Herbert) died in the Boer War; but (as he
does in *A Shropshire Lad* and in *Last Poems*) Housman allows the issue to
increase in significance until the problem of dead soldiers becomes an
instance of the problem of dead humanity—"the perished nation."

Like many poems in *A Shropshire Lad*, poem XXVI in *More Poems*
speaks positively of suicide. Also like several poems in *A Shropshire Lad*,
poem XXIV presents the death of a lover in terms of faithlessness. The
image of life as a treadmill, from *A Shropshire Lad* LV, returns here as
well: in XXVII all of the options or chances for humanity, forever, are
summarized in two lines—"To stand up straight and tread the turning

mill, / To lie flat and know nothing and be still." And the Epicureanism of Housman's poetry is presented as clearly and forcibly here as anywhere in all of his work:

> Come to the stolen waters,
>> And leap the guarded pale,
> And pull the flower in season
>> Before desire shall fail.
>
> It shall not last for ever,
>> No more than earth and skies;
> But he that drinks in season
>> Shall live before he dies. (XXII)

The fact that desire's object is "stolen" in that poem is connected with another feature of *More Poems* (and the series *Additional Poems*, 18 of which Laurence published in his memoir, *My Brother, A. E. Housman*) that has received perhaps more emphasis in Housman studies than it deserves. As if they had assumed that readers were more interested in the sex life of the person than the work of the poet, some commentators have written as if Laurence Housman had chosen and published poems that expressed his brother's homosexuality. It would be possible (but pointless) to interpret *More Poems* XXXI, for example, as an expression of Housman's unrequited homosexual love for Moses Jackson, and the poem on the death of Moses's younger brother Adalbert (poem XLII) has predictably produced speculation that Housman may have had homosexual feelings about him, too. In *Additional Poems*, II ("Oh were he and I together") could be interpreted as an expression of homosexual feeling, though its meaning emerges rather in the last stanza: "Kingdoms are for others' plunder, / And content for other slain."

If one were interested in gossip rather than poetic art, one could interpret *Additional Poems* VI as if it were about secret homosexual feelings: "Ask me no more, for fear I should reply"; but its meaning, too, involves another and a larger issue, as its last stanza makes plain: "all are slain." Poem XIV of *Additional Poems* states its larger subject explicitly enough: "the jar of nations, / The noise of a world run mad." Reductive interpretations which allege that the poems express chiefly personal (homosexual) feelings, which Housman otherwise kept secret, mistake a

major poetic achievement for autobiography or gossip; such mistakes
should not be allowed to mislead readers or to distract them from the
book's artistry and intellectual importance.

One of the poems' themes is precisely the maturation *from* the trivial-
ity of personal love-feelings (as per the true-love scripts of popular entertainment): for example, *More Poems* XXXVII positively ridicules and
repudiates such conventional fictions about true love. The poem begins
"I did not lose my heart in summer's even," and goes on to voice the
superior reality of feelings about more important subjects, including war,
and the misery and death that it produces. Poem XLI narrates an incident in which a street beggar reminds the speaker of another man—
someone who died long ago, over the sea. Like *A Shropshire Lad, More
Poems* develops this dual theme—the antiwar theme and the Epicurean
theme of desire doomed by mortality—with critiques of illusion (including propaganda and religious fictions). The artistry with which these
themes are orchestrated, in the coherence of the poetic volume, is (as I
have said) Laurence's work; but the artistry with which they are developed inside the poems themselves is Housman's poetic achievement.

Chapter Six

Conclusion

Suitably for the work of a professed Cyrenaic, Housman's poetry can afford (and for generations *has* afforded) great pleasure: in his poems the artistry of music, image, language, and form are extraordinary, as I have tried to suggest in earlier chapters in this book; feelings and the fiction of feelings are composed in his poems with rare craft. Beyond the indulgence of readerly hedonism (enjoyment for enjoyment's sake), his work has considerable intellectual depth, as I have also tried to show. As Housman argued about the scholarly work of textual criticism, the *application* of thought is crucially important, and not only the enjoyment of what one takes to be an *author's* thought. One can momentarily enjoy the fiction of what a character "feels," and one can momentarily enjoy the illusion that there is present in a poem the author's "thought" which he has therein "expressed"; but Housman's life's work involved him in the handling and analysis of documents (and not only "ideas"). His daily work was the study of how documents (which are physical objects) are produced, reproduced, changed, transmitted, and used.

The difference between what a person once thought and what a document now says is the crucial ground of Housman's voluminous work as a scholar, which he pursued industriously for 54 years, from his first published essay, which was on a text by Horace, until the week of his death, when he was still lecturing on classical literature and scholarship at Cambridge. From his work in prose and verse we can learn much, and much more than what he meant.

I hope it is now clear that (for example) his poetry reveals beautifully how historical conflicts are refracted in poems that seem innocent of them: his poems that are harshly critical of the queen and of imperial war and his poems that are likewise critical about widespread prejudices and legal persecution present lyrically lovely surfaces. And from this feature of all of his poetry, from his first book onward, we learn more: we learn about suppression, in more ways than one. His poems show how dangerous content (politically dangerous fantasies about the death of a queen, for example, and legally dangerous fantasies about forbidden practices ["stolen waters"]) is suppressed *outwardly*, in the machinery of prohibition that simply prevents the appearance of such content in plain English print, and *inwardly*, in the buried life of metaphor, symbol, and irony that conceals its danger behind a safely straight face.

Further, Housman's poetry shows with rare clarity and trenchancy how dangerous *conceptual* content (as opposed to topical or political contentions) can be preserved in the artful submergence of poems. Friedrich Nietzsche argued (for example, in *Beyond Good and Evil*) that moral systems are hollow fictions, often used by the powerful to repress and oppress deluded people; and Nietzsche's arguments are written to be and to seem outrageous. Their outrageous character has placed them in the harmless periphery of culture, where marginalized intellectuals live and where (roped off from the realities of social power) they cannot really threaten the effectiveness of the propaganda that comforts us. In contrast, Housman's poems, which suggest that moral systems are hollow fictions used by the powerful to repress and oppress deluded people, are written to seem *not* outrageous, and they have been reproduced in the centers of culture, where everybody lives. They have even been reproduced and distributed by the bureaucratic war machinery that their lovely singsong attacks. His ridicule of patriotism and patriotic death has been used as propaganda *for* patriotism and patriotic death. His ridicule of the meaningless excitements of futile sports as so many rehearsals for the meaningless excitement of futile war has been enjoyed by thousands of excited sports fans and patriotic soldiers.

To compare a critique of religious delusion and prejudice by Ludwig Feuerbach or Benjamin Jowett with Housman's critiques of religious delusion and prejudice (as in "The Oracles" or "When Israel out of Egypt came") is to learn much about the artifice of safe surfaces and dangerous depths. The work of Feuerbach and of Jowett has been consigned to the harmless periphery of culture, where only intellectuals live; Housman's poems have been reproduced and distributed in the very same ideological state apparatuses (for example, schools and universities) whose machinery of propaganda he criticizes.

When Housman did write of such issues in clear prose (as opposed to the artful symbolism of his poems), he made these differences, and his understanding of them, quite clear as well. For example, the inaugural lecture which he delivered at Cambridge, on the occasion of his appointment as Kennedy Professor of Latin, is entirely explicit about the historicity of prejudices, the falsehood of conventional forms of thought, and the oppression—even the specifically political oppression—which that system of prejudice and conventional falsehood supports. Even in connection with factual scholarship and hard science, Housman writes that it is not truth but comfort (even comfortable delusions) that is commonly preferred (*Confines*, 27–28).

He writes of historical relativity too, advising that one should "consider the mutations of opinion, the reversals of literary judgment, which this one small island has witnessed in the last 150 years: what is the likelihood that your notions or your contemporaries' notions of the exquisite are those of a foreigner who wrote for foreigners two millenniums ago?"; he says that we must learn to be suspicious of our own preferences, our own tastes, our own judgments (*Confines*, 34). Housman's skepticism—like Bertrand Russell's skepticism—includes the recognition that it is generally not truth but rather wishes and desires that determine what people "believe": people "hate to feel insecure; and a sense of security depends much less on the correctness of our opinions than on the firmness with which we hold them"; too frequently, Housman suggests, a student asks of a teacher—or any follower asks of a leader—"not *tell me how to get rid of error* but *tell me how to get rid of doubt*" (*Confines*, 40). Thus are developed "the mental habits of the slave" (*Confines*, 42), who "believes that the fashion of the present, unlike all fashions heretofore, will endure perpetually, and that its own flimsy tabernacle of secondhand opinions is a habitation for everlasting." Housman writes thus of "the stiff and self-righteous arrogance of the unthinking man" (*Confines*, 43), and he quotes Francis Bacon's observation that "the mind of man is . . . full of superstition and imposture" (*Confines*, 44). He does not deny that popular illusions are comforting; he denies, instead, that they are *true*. Further, he suggests that popular illusions (like religion and patriotism, the officially distributed ideological illusions of which his poems are critical) have the *political* effect of keeping oppressed people in their (oppressed) place: "this is the felicity of the house of bondage" (*Confines*, 43).

As I have said, however, the application of thought to Housman's work involves (or should involve) much more than stating all over again what *he* consciously "thought" or what he "meant" to "express": if his work is to teach us more than to reproduce already existing thoughts (true, false, or otherwise), if it is to cultivate mental habits *other* than those of slaves, and if it is to take us *out* of the house of bondage, which is the house of conventional prejudice, we must learn to understand what his work reveals beyond his consciously professed intentions. The production and reproduction of texts, the means by which preferred meanings are socially promulgated, the social and political *use* of texts and meanings, and the fact that there is something fictitious about our conventional mental habits, including our illusions about poetry and how it works—these are large and important issues into which the study of Housman's poems can lead. An example that will at first appear to be a detail may help to illustrate how these larger issues arise.

Housman never permitted the publication of his Cambridge inaugural lecture, because in it he reported a fact that he was unable later to confirm. In the lecture Housman insists on the difference between, on the one hand, the appreciations that are composed by literary critics and enjoyed by audiences and, on the other hand, the factual and material truth, as in texts which are (in fact) physical objects. He had produced (*Confines*, 31–33) an example from the poetry of Shelley, quoting a line "which was printed, and is known by heart to hundreds of thousands" in this form: "Fresh Spring, and Summer, and Winter hoar." Housman points out that the line has nine syllables rather than the ten syllables which the poem's verse requires, and "it mentions three seasons instead of four." He points out that one editor (William Michael Rossetti) corrected the line to read as follows: "Fresh Spring and Summer, Autumn, Winter hoar." He then quotes Swinburne's defense of the traditional form of the line as a verse of "more divine and sovereign sweetness than any other" and as "a thing to thrill the veins and draw tears to the eyes of all" who are not deaf.

Housman then observes that Shelley actually wrote "with his own hand 'Fresh Spring and Autumn, Summer and Winter hoar.'" He remarks wrily but justly that "the one verse . . . of more divine and sovereign sweetness than any other is the verse, not of Shelley, but of a compositor": it was a worker in a print shop who produced the melodious excellence that Swinburne admired; "Mr. Swinburne's veins were thrilled, and tears were drawn to Mr. Swinburne's eyes, by a misprint."[1]

The importance and meaning of this example are more than the mere fact of a textual mistake on Swinburne's part: the example means that all texts which we can hold in our hands are material products; texts are not personal *intentions*. The example means that the production of a text is an act, and that interpretations and appreciations are then acts in their own right. A text is nonidentical with its "meaning." "It" is not identical with what it "means." Housman's arguments in textual criticism include the contention that it is not always true that the best (most sensible, most meaningful) readings are correct and that more difficult (less apparently meaningful) readings are incorrect (see *Prose*, 35–36). He argues for the necessity of basing judgment on evidential grounds rather than one's fondness for meaning. He observes that the popular (almost universal) fondness for meaning has produced errors and corruptions, and (as a rule) the fondness for meaning *will* produce error and corruption.

It is impossible to do the sort of scholarly work that Housman did, every day, without discovering the difference between (1) a literary work (which is a document) and (2) what it "means." It is also impossible to do that sort of work, every day, without discovering how totally time, custom, prejudice, fashion, law, politics, power, superstition, and belief *change* both works and meanings. These, too, are meanings which Housman's works can reveal.

Notes and References

Preface

1. In recent years this point of view has been expressed influentially in several books by Jerome J. McGann: *A Critique of Modern Textual Criticism* (Chicago: University of Chicago Press, 1983); *The Romantic Ideology* (Chicago: University of Chicago Press, 1983); *The Beauty of Inflections* (Oxford: Oxford University Press, 1985); *Social Values and Poetic Acts* (Cambridge, Mass.: Harvard University Press, 1988); and *Toward a Literature of Knowledge* (Chicago: University of Chicago Press, 1989).

2. Greene, "Housman Since 1936: Popular Responses and Professional Revaluations in America," *Housman Society Journal* 12 (1986): 30–31; hereafter cited in text and notes.

3. For example, *Alfred Edward Housman* (Bromsgrove: Bromsgrove School, 1936): this volume is a collection of reminiscences of Housman by Katharine E. Symons (his sister), A. W. Pollard (a friend from his undergraduate days), Laurence Housman, R. W. Chambers (a student at University College London when Housman was Professor of Latin there), Alan Ker, A. S. F. Gow, John Sparrow, and N. V. H. Symons; hereafter cited in text and notes as Symons. This collection of reminiscences of Housman was reprinted in the following year, as *Alfred Edward Housman* (New York: Henry Holt & Co., 1937). Another important book that appeared shortly after the poet's death is Laurence Housman, *A. E. H.: Some Poems, Some Letters and a Personal Memoir By His Brother Laurence Housman* (London: Jonathan Cape, 1937); this book was reprinted as *My Brother, A. E. Housman: Personal Recollections Together with Thirty Hitherto Unpublished Poems* (New York: Charles Scribner's Sons, 1938); hereafter cited in text and notes as L. Housman 1938. Yet another major work is Grant Richards, *Housman 1897–1936* (London: Oxford University Press, 1941); hereafter cited in text and notes.

4. Two recent examples are Keith Jebb, *A. E. Housman* (Mid Glamorgan: Seren Books, 1992), and John Bayley, *Housman's Poems* (Oxford: Clarendon Press, 1992). Both works are hereafter cited in text.

5. On this controversy, see Tom Burns Haber, *The Manuscript Poems of A. E. Housman: Eight Hundred Lines of Hitherto Uncollected Verse from the Author's Notebooks* (Oxford: Oxford University Press, 1955); John Sparrow, "The Housman Dilemma," *Times Literary Supplement*, 29 April 1955, 189–91; William White, "A. E. Housman: A Critical and Bibliographical Review of Books About the Poet, 1936–1955," *Journal of English and Germanic Philology* 56 (1957): 246; and Greene, 38–40. All of these works are hereafter cited in text and notes.

6. Some controversy, for example, arose over Maude M. Hawkins's biography, *A. E. Housman: Man Behind a Mask* (Chicago: Henry Regnery, 1958). More recently, there has been disputation between two other biographers, Richard Perceval Graves and Norman Page: see Graves, *A. E. Housman The Scholar-Poet* (London: Routledge and Kegan Paul, 1979); Page, *A. E. Housman: A Critical Biography* (New York: Schocken, 1983); and Graves, "Biography and A. E. Housman," *Housman Society Journal*, 12 (1986): 15–21. All of these works are hereafter cited in text and notes.

7. On the writing of biography, and on this set of issues especially, see three recent books by Reed Whittemore: *Pure Lives: The Early Biographers* (Baltimore: Johns Hopkins University Press, 1988); *Whole Lives: Shapers of Modern Biography* (Baltimore: Johns Hopkins University Press, 1989); and *Six Literary Lives: The Shared Impiety of Adams, London, Sinclair, Williams, Dos Passos, and Tate* (Columbia: University of Missouri Press, 1993).

Chapter One

1. A. W. Pollard, "Some Reminiscences," in Symons, 31; R. W. Chambers, "A London Memoir," in Symons, 44. Graves quotes a letter from E. W. Watson dated 25 May 1936 and located now at Trinity College, Cambridge, indicating that in his college years Housman had memorized much of Matthew Arnold's poetry: "Housman would challenge us to cite a line the continuation of which he could not give. We never caught him out" (quoted in Graves 1979, 40).

Laurence Housman writes that "Matthew Arnold he placed high: both as critic and as an interpreter of human life in its relation to the Powers Above"; he specifies *Empedocles on Etna* and a "poem, which was one of his own (Housman's) favourites, addressed to an unsuccessful soldier in the war of liberation of humanity,

> Creep into thy narrow bed,
> Creep, and let no more be said!
> Vain thy onset! all stands fast;
> Thou thyself must break at last."

See L. Housman 1938, 67–68.

2. Arnold, "The Buried Life," first published in *Empedocles on Etna and Other Poems* (1852); reprinted in *Matthew Arnold* (Oxford Authors), ed. Miriam Allott and Robert H. Super (Oxford: Oxford University Press, 1986), 153.

3. Housman, letter to Maurice Pollet, 5 February 1933, in *The Letters of A. E. Housman*, ed. Henry Maas (London: Rupert Hart-Davis, 1971), 328; hereafter cited in text and notes as *Letters*.

4. Unless otherwise indicated, biographical information about Housman is summarized in the present chapter from the following sources:

Letters; Symons; L. Housman 1938; Richards; Graves 1979; Page; Tom Burns Haber, *A. E. Housman* (New York: Twayne, 1967) (hereafter cited in text and notes); and John Pugh, *Bromsgrove and the Housmans* (Bromsgrove: The Housman Society, 1974); hereafter cited in text and notes.

     5.   Laurence Housman, letter to Maude Hawkins, 6 August 1950; Library of Congress. Quoted by Page, 23.

     6.   Laurence Housman, *The Unexpected Years* (Indianapolis: Bobbs-Merrill, 1936), 62; hereafter cited in text as L. Housman 1936; quoted by Page, 25.

     7.   Lucy Housman, diary for 24 July 1882; quoted by Page, 26–27.

     8.   See V. H. H. Green, *A History of Oxford University* (London: B. T. Batsford, 1974).

     9.   Housman, annotation in a book by A. E. Taylor on Greek philosophy, quoted by Graves 1979, 48.

    10.   Chambers, *Vestiges of the Natural History of Creation*, quoted by J. A. V. Chapple, *Science and Literature in the Nineteenth Century* (Houndmills and London: Macmillan, 1986), 69.

    11.   Algernon Charles Swinburne, "The Garden of Proserpine," in *Poems and Ballads* (1866), reprinted in *The New Oxford Book of Victorian Verse*, ed. Christopher Ricks (Oxford: Oxford University Press, 1987), 389–91; hereafter cited in text and notes.

    12.   Swinburne, "A Forsaken Garden," first published in *Athenaeum*, 22 July 1876, reprinted in Ricks 1987, 393.

    13.   For Housman's arguments about textual criticism, see for example his preface to the first volume of his edition of Manilius, *Astronomica* (1903), reprinted in *"The Name and Nature of Poetry" and Other Selected Prose*, ed. John Carter (1961; reprinted New York: New Amsterdam Books, 1989), 23–44; and his "The Application of Thought to Textual Criticism" (1921), reprinted in *"The Name and Nature of Poetry" and Other Selected Prose*, 131–150. Hereafter this volume will be identified in the short form, *Prose*.

    14.   Lucretius, *On the Nature of the Universe* (*De Rerum Natura*), translated by R. E. Latham (1951; reprinted Middlesex: Penguin, 1981), 28, 51, 99; hereafter cited in text.

    15.   Housman's "Iona" was first published in 1961 in *A. E. Housman: A Collection of Manuscripts, Letters, Proofs, First Editions, Etc. Formed by H. B. Collamore . . . Presented to the Lilly Library, Indiana University. Exhibition April 1–30, 1961*, 5. The poem is reprinted in an appendix in Pugh, xviii–xxiv, from which my quotations are taken.

    16.   Housman, "A Morning with the Royal Family," quoted by Graves 1979, 39.

    17.   A. S. F. Gow, *A. E. Housman: A Sketch* (Cambridge: Cambridge University Press, 1936), 5.

    18.   Walter L. Arnstein, *Britain Yesterday and Today: 1830 to the Present* (Boston: D. C. Heath, 1966), 138.

19. Laurence Housman, *Alfred Edward Housman's "De Amicitia": An Account written by Laurence Housman of his brother Alfred's Life . . . Deposited with the British Museum Department of Manuscripts by Laurence Housman in May 1942* (London: Little Rabbit Book Co., 1976), 22–23; hereafter cited in text as L. Housman 1976.

20. Laurence Housman to Maude Hawkins, 21 July 1958, quoted by Page, 53.

21. A very short but useful account of the history of homosexuality is Chris Waters, "Homosexuality," in *Victorian Britain: An Encyclopedia*, ed. Sally Mitchell (New York: Garland, 1988), 371–73.

22. Crompton, *Byron and Greek Love: Homophobia in Nineteenth-Century England* (Berkeley: University of California Press, 1985), 14–25, 45–46; hereafter cited in text.

23. For an account of these issues in the period, see Jeffrey Weeks, *Coming Out: Homosexual Politics in Britain, from the Nineteenth Century to the Present* (London: Quartet Books, 1977); Weeks discusses Laurence Housman's work in this connection, e.g., 124, 128, 134.

24. Letter from Katharine Symons to A. S. F. Gow, 15 June 1936, now located at Trinity College, Cambridge, quoted by Page, 47.

Chapter Two

1. *Letters*, 267; for Wilde's response, see Graves 1979, 113.

2. In his preface to the published text of his play, *Pains and Penalties*, for example, Laurence Housman reports that his play had been condemned and censored by the Lord Chamberlain, because the play contained "unfavourable comments on the character of King George IV" (*Pains and Penalties: The Defence of Queen Caroline. A Play in Four Acts* [London: Sidgwick & Jackson, 1911], v).

3. Ralph Griffin, a colleague of Housman at the Patent Office, writes in a letter of 1936 (to A. F. Scholfield) that he did not know, while he worked at Housman's side, that Housman was a scholar: see Page, 51 and n.

4. R. W. Chambers, *Man's Unconquerable Mind: Studies of English Writers from Bede to A. E. Housman and W. P. Ker* (1939; reprinted London: Jonathan Cape, 1964), 370. Chambers had been a student of Housman's at University College and later joined the faculty there.

5. For a list of some of the reviews, a summary of information about the editions, and some information about musical settings of the book, see Graves 1979, 114–17. John Carter and John Sparrow indicate that the fourth edition appeared in 1903, whereas Graves and Page (Page, 86) indicate 1902: see Carter and Sparrow, *A. E. Housman: A Bibliography* (Godalming, Surrey: St. Paul's Bibliographies, 1982), 8.

6. Quotations from Housman's poetry refer to *The Collected Poems of A. E. Housman* (New York: Henry Holt, 1965).

7. Simonides, "Uncertainty of Life" (translated anonymously), in *Collections from the Greek Anthology*, ed. Robert Bland (London: John Murray, 1813), 185.

8. This anecdote, from a letter in the 5 May 1936 *Times*, is reproduced in Richards, 289, and again in Page, 111.

9. Horace, *Odes*, Book 1, Ode 4, in *Horace: The Odes and Epodes*, translated by C. E. Bennett, rev. ed. (1927; reprinted Cambridge: Harvard University Press; London: William Heinemann, 1978), 17. This is the edition in the Loeb Classical Library.

10. Dowson's poem is conveniently reproduced in Ricks 1987, 584.

11. Asklepiades, "To His Mistress," from *Poems from the Greek Anthology*, translated by Dudley Fitts (New York: New Directions, 1956), 35.

12. Eliot, "Tradition and the Individual Talent" (1919), in *Selected Essays* (New York: Harcourt, Brace and World, 1964), 4.

13. Pater, conclusion to *The Renaissance* (first published in 1873), cited here from *The Renaissance: Studies in Art and Poetry. The 1893 Text*, ed. Donald L. Hill (Berkeley: University of California Press, 1980), 62, 190.

14. See especially Hoagwood, "Classical Scepticism in the Poetry of A. E. Housman," *Housman Society Journal*, 14 (1988): 19–28.

15. Tom Burns Haber, *The Making of "A Shropshire Lad": A Manuscript Variorum* (Seattle: University of Washington Press, 1966), 35; hereinafter cited in text and notes.

16. On these historical developments, see H. C. G. Matthew, "The Liberal Age," in *The Oxford History of Britain*, ed. Kenneth O. Morgan (Oxford: Oxford University Press, 1988), 560–64; hereafter cited in text.

17. Eliot, review of "The Name and Nature of Poetry," *Criterion*, 13, no. 50 (Oct. 1933): 152.

Chapter Three

1. *The Confines of Criticism: The Cambridge Inaugural 1911* (Cambridge: Cambridge University Press, 1969); hereafter cited in text and notes as *Confines*.

2. Withers' statement, which appeared in the 9 May 1936 *New Statesman*, is quoted in L. Housman 1938, 97.

3. Housman's statement appears in a letter to Henry Holland, quoted in Page, 114.

4. See the "Complete List of Dated Poems" in L. Housman 1938, 273–75.

Chapter Four

1. For the poems in *A Shropshire Lad*, Housman used roman numerals as titles; for a few poems, however, he added a verbal title (for example, poem XXVII, "The Welsh Marches"). It is conventional to refer to the poems by roman numeral and verbal title in those cases in which Housman supplied such

a title, and to refer to the other poems in the collection by roman numeral and opening phrase (for example, poem II, "Loveliest of trees"). Sometimes the poems have been reproduced without the numeral, as if the opening phrase *were* a title ("Loveliest of Trees"). Though different methods of reference are widely used, it is always easy to identify the poem under discussion.

2.   As early as 1898, for example, William Archer wrote that he found in *A Shropshire Lad* "an exultant patriotism" (*A. E. Housman: The Critical Heritage*, ed. Philip Gardner [London: Routledge, 1992] 77; hereafter cited in text and notes), which is a testimony to the triumph of Housman's irony.

3.   Leggett, *Housman's Land of Lost Content: A Critical Study of "A Shropshire Lad"* (Knoxville: University of Tennessee Press, 1970), 79; hereafter cited in text and notes.

4.   Brooks, "Alfred Edward Housman" (1959), reprinted in *A. E. Housman: A Collection of Critical Essays*, ed. Christopher Ricks (Englewood Cliffs, NJ: Prentice-Hall, 1968), 75; hereafter cited in text and notes.

5.   In Haber 1966, the author indicates that the draft of the poem was written in April or May, 1895: see 34.

6.   Leggett, *The Poetic Art of A. E. Housman* (Lincoln: University of Nebraska Press, 1978), 47–49.

7.   R. T. R., "Housman's 'Farewell to Barn and Stack and Tree,'" *The Explicator*, 1 (1942–43), Item 36; and Leggett 1970, 22–23.

8.   Tinker, "Housman's Poetry," *Yale Review* (1935); reprinted in Gardner, 265.

9.   On cyclical imagery and structure in Housman's poems, see Tom Burns Haber, "A. E. Housman: Astronomer-Poet," *English Studies* 35 (1954): 154–58; and Leggett 1970, 39–46.

10.   Leavis and Thompson, *Culture and Environment* (1933; reprinted London: Chatto and Windus, 1964), 73, 84, 87, 91, 95–96.

11.   Brooks, "Alfred Edward Housman" (1959), reprinted in Ricks 1968; Leggett quotes this passage (Leggett 1978, 19), but does not otherwise comment on the poem, but in his earlier book Leggett had written of the poem in ways that agree with Brooks' paraphrase (Leggett 1970, 57–58).

12.   It may be that mistaking the grimness of the humor is what led one otherwise good critic to mistake and condemn the poem as "comic surfeit . . . at its worst": Morton Dauwen Zabel, "The Whole of Housman," *Nation* 90 (1 June 1940); reprinted in Gardner, 396. Perhaps for similar reasons, several otherwise good critics pass the poem by in complete silence: e.g., Leggett 1970 and 1978, and Bayley.

13.   Gabriel García Márquez, "Death Constant Beyond Love," in *Collected Stories* (New York: Harper and Row, 1984), 238.

14.   See Bertrand Russell, *Sceptical Essays* (1956; reprinted London: Unwin, 1977), 19, 23–24, and 46.

15.   For example, Charles Sorley, whose paper on Housman (calling him

"startlingly stoical") is reproduced in *The Letters of Charles Sorley* (Cambridge University Press, 1919), 48–53, and again in Gardner, 93–97.

16. *Handbook of Epictetus*, translated by Nicholas White (Indianapolis: Hackett, 1983), 16.

17. Munro, *Some Contemporary Poets* (1920); reprinted in Gardner, 110.

Chapter Five

1. The quoted phrases appear in reviews by an anonymous writer in the *Times Literary Supplement* of 19 October 1922; by Edmund Gosse writing in the *Sunday Times* for 22 October 1922; by J. C. Squire writing in the *London Mercury* of November 1922; and by Amabel Williams-Ellis writing in *Spectator* for 4 November 1922; see Gardner, 112, 116, 124, 127.

2. See the "Chronology of the Poems" in *Complete Poems: A. E. Housman. Centennial Edition*, with an Introduction by Basil Davenport and a "History of the Text" by Tom Burns Haber (New York: Henry Holt & Co., 1959), 257–60; this chronology is based on the earlier one composed by Laurence Housman and published in L. Housman 1938.

3. Greene, 34; and William White, "A. E. Housman: An Annotated Check-List. Additions and Corrections: III," *Library* 7 (September 1952): 207.

4. Laurence Housman, "Preface" to *More Poems* (New York: Alfred A. Knopf, 1936), vi–vii.

5. Terence Allan Hoagwood, "Poetic Design in *More Poems*," *Housman Society Journal*, 12 (1986): 84; hereafter cited in text.

Chapter Six

1. Housman had read of the textual problem in Shelley's poem in an article which he could not later locate or identify, and for this reason he prevented the publication of his lecture. In his edition of *The Confines of Criticism*, John Carter reproduces the surviving manuscript versions of Shelley's line, showing that Shelley had at one time written the word "autumn" in the line, and then revised the line leaving a large space in which to insert another word. Shelley died without publishing (or completing) the poem; Mary Shelley published it after Shelley's death, sending the printer a copy in which the empty space was increased, to emphasize the fact that there was a missing word—intended and necessary to complete the line, but still missing. The printer (not Shelley) then made the line that Swinburne admired. As Carter says, "Housman, in short, was right" (p. 54).

Selected Bibliography

PRIMARY WORKS

Poetry

A Shropshire Lad. London: Kegan Paul, 1896. [Second edition is *A Shropshire Lad*. London: Grant Richards, 1898.]
Last Poems. London: Grant Richards, 1922.
More Poems. [Assembled by Laurence Housman after the poet's death.] London: Jonathan Cape, 1936. [Simultaneous American Edition: *More Poems*. New York: Knopf, 1936.]
Selected Poems. New York: Editions for the Armed Services, n.d. [1942?].
Complete Poems: A. E. Housman. Centennial Edition. With an Introduction by Basil Davenport and a History of the Text by Tom Burns Haber. New York: Henry Holt & Co., 1959.
The Collected Poems of A. E. Housman. New York: Henry Holt, 1965.

Prose

Introductory Lecture Delivered Before the Faculties of Arts and of Science in University College, London, October 3, 1892, by A. E. Housman. Cambridge: Printed at the University Press, 1892.
The Name and Nature of Poetry . . . The Leslie Stephen Lecture Delivered at Cambridge 9 May 1933. Cambridge: Cambridge University Press, 1933.
The Confines of Criticism: The Cambridge Inaugural 1911. Ed. John Carter. Cambridge: Cambridge University Press, 1969.
The Letters of A. E. Housman. Edited by Henry Maas. London: Rupert Hart-Davis, 1971.
"The Name and Nature of Poetry" and Other Selected Prose. Edited by John Carter. 1961. Reprinted New York: New Amsterdam Books, 1989.

Scholarly Writing (Latin)

M. Manilii Astronomicon . . . recensuit et enarravit A. E. Housman. Editio altera. Cantabrigiae, Typis Academiae, 1937. (Housman's edition of Manilius, which he intended as his scholarly monument.)
D. Ivvnalis Saturae editorum in usum edidit A. E. Housman. Cantabrigiae, Typis Academiae, 1931. (Housman's edition of Juvenal.)
The Classical Papers of A. E. Housman. Edited by J. Diggle and F. R. D. Goodyear. 3 vols. Cambridge: Cambridge University Press, 1972.

SECONDARY WORKS: WORKS ABOUT HOUSMAN, AND
OTHER HISTORICAL AND LITERARY WORKS CITED

Arnold, Matthew. *Matthew Arnold*. Oxford Authors Series. Edited by Miriam
    Allott and Robert H. Super. Oxford: Oxford University Press, 1986. A
    good and easily available edition of works by one of Housman's favorite
    nineteenth-century poets.
Arnstein, Walter L. *Britain Yesterday and Today: 1830 to the Present*. Boston: D.
    C. Heath, 1966. A history of the period, recommended especially for stu-
    dents.
Bayley, John. *Housman's Poems*. Oxford: Clarendon Press, 1992. A general study
    of Housman's poems, and a critical introduction to his work.
Bland, Robert, ed. *Collections from the Greek Anthology*. London: John Murray,
    1813. Selections, in English translation, from the most influential anthol-
    ogy of ancient lyrics, with which Housman's poems are frequently com-
    parable in subject and tone.
Carter, John and John Sparrow. *A. E. Housman: A Bibliography*. Second Edition.
    Revised by William White. Godalming, Surrey: St. Paul's Bibliographies,
    1982. A revision of *A. E. Housman: An Annotated Hand-List* which had
    appeared in 1940.
Chambers, R. W. *Man's Unconquerable Mind: Studies of English Writers from Bede
    to A. E. Housman and W. P. Ker*. 1939. Reprinted London: Jonathan Cape,
    1964. Chambers had been a student at University College, University of
    London, where Housman taught; later he joined the faculty there; and he
    was a friend of Housman's of very long standing, as well as a literary crit-
    ic. His reminiscences are valuable as sympathetic observations by a con-
    temporary.
Chapple, J. A. V. *Science and Literature in the Nineteenth Century*. Houndmills and
    London: Macmillan, 1986. A valuable source on developments in such
    sciences as biological evolution, and their cultural importance.
Crompton, Louis. *Byron and Greek Love: Homophobia in Nineteenth-Century
    England*. Berkeley: University of California Press, 1985. Includes much
    valuable information about homosexuality in the nineteenth century,
    including its persecution and punishment.
Eliot, T. S. Review of "The Name and Nature of Poetry." *The Criterion* 13, no.
    50 (Oct. 1933): 151–54. High praise of Housman's essay, by one of the
    most influential poets of the twentieth century.
————. *Selected Essays*. New York: Harcourt, Brace and World, 1964.
    Influential literary essays, including "Tradition and the Individual
    Talent."
Epictetus. *Handbook of Epictetus*. Translated by Nicholas White. Indianapolis:
    Hackett, 1983. One of the central texts of classical Stoicism.

Fitts, Dudley, trans. *Poems from the Greek Anthology*. New York: New Directions, 1956. A different selection of poems, in translation, from the same anthology as Bland's (above).

García Márquez, Gabriel. *Collected Stories*. New York: Harper and Row, 1984. A collection of stories by one of the world's foremost writers, including "Death Constant Beyond Love," which includes an allusion to (and implicitly an interpretation of) a poem by Housman.

Gardner, Philip, ed. *A. E. Housman: The Critical Heritage*. London: Routledge, 1992. Reprints reviews and critical essays ranging in date from 1896 through 1951. Useful introductory essay by Gardner on the history of critical responses to Housman's poetry.

Gow, A. S. F. *A. E. Housman: A Sketch*. Cambridge: Cambridge University Press, 1936. An early and good biographical account, by a scholar who knew Housman.

Graves, Richard Perceval. *A. E. Housman The Scholar-Poet*. London: Routledge and Kegan Paul, 1979. One of the most important biographies of the poet in recent decades.

———. "Biography and A. E. Housman." *Housman Society Journal*, 12 (1986): 15–21. Part of a dialogue, in books and essays, between Graves and Norman Page (see below), concerning Housman's life and alternative interpretations of it.

Green, V. H. H. *A History of Oxford University*. London: B. T. Batsford, 1974. Useful source of information about the university that Housman attended, issues that were current at the time, and scholars who were prominent when Housman was there.

Greene, Ghussan R. "Housman Since 1936: Popular Responses and Professional Revaluations in America." *Housman Society Journal* 12 (1986): 30–46. An account of formal and informal responses to Housman's life and work, including anecdotes and some scholarly studies.

Haber, Tom Burns. "A. E. Housman: Astronomer-Poet," *English Studies* 35 (1954): 154–58. On cyclical imagery and structure in Housman's poems.

———. *The Manuscript Poems of A. E. Housman: Eight Hundred Lines of Hitherto Uncollected Verse from the Author's Notebooks*. Oxford: Oxford University Press, 1955. Transcription of poetry from the unpublished notebooks of Housman, located at the Library of Congress.

———. *The Making of "A Shropshire Lad": A Manuscript Variorum*. Seattle: University of Washington Press, 1966. A transcription of the drafts of the 63 poems in *A Shropshire Lad*, from Housman's notebooks. Haber adds commentaries on the composition of the poems and of the book.

———. *A. E. Housman*. New York: Twayne, 1967. A general biographical and critical study, recommended especially for students.

Hawkins, Maude M. *A. E. Housman: Man Behind a Mask*. Chicago: Henry Regnery, 1958. A biography that has produced some controversy. This

book includes letters written by Housman, for some of which Hawkins's
book is the only source. (In such a case, Maas's edition, listed above, uses
Hawkins's text.)

Hoagwood, Terence Allan. "Poetic Design in *More Poems*: Laurence and A. E.
Housman. Part One." *Housman Society Journal* 12 (1986): 77–86. "Three
strategies unify the volume . . .: patterns of imagistic and thematic development. . . . Second, an estrangement of assertion. . . . And, finally, an
ethos of sympathy."

———. "Poetic Design in *More Poems*: Part Two." *Housman Society Journal* 13
(1987): 7–13. "The irony of sceptical assertion and denial, the imagistic
coherence of the book as a whole, and the ethos of sympathy that provides a moral theme belong to the classical literature to which Housman
devoted his professional life."

———. "Classical Scepticism in the Poetry of A. E. Housman." *Housman Society
Journal*, 14 (1988): 19–28. With reference to ancient skeptics including
Horace and Cicero, and with reference to Housman's scholarly work on
these Latin authors, this essay shows how classical figures of speech and
thought, including the "dreamer hypothesis," contribute to the "intellectual seriousness and emotional depth of the poems."

Horace. *The Odes and Epodes*, translated by C. E. Bennett. Rev. ed. 1927.
Reprinted Cambridge: Harvard University Press; London: William
Heinemann, 1978. This is the Loeb Classical Library edition. The Latin
texts and English translations appear on facing pages.

Housman, Laurence. *Pains and Penalties: The Defence of Queen Caroline. A Play in
Four Acts.* London: Sidgwick & Jackson, 1911. A play on an important
political conflict of the nineteenth century, with a preface by Laurence
Housman on the problem of governmental censorship.

———. *The Unexpected Years.* Indianapolis: Bobbs-Merrill, 1936. Contains
some letters and poems by A. E. Housman, first published in this
book.

———. *A. E. H.: Some Poems, Some Letters and a Personal Memoir By His Brother
Laurence Housman.* London: Jonathan Cape, 1937. This book was reprinted as *My Brother, A. E. Housman: Personal Recollections Together with Thirty
Hitherto Unpublished Poems.* New York: Charles Scribner's Sons, 1938. An
important biography. Most of the poems included here had never been
published before.

———. *Alfred Edward Housman's "De Amicitia": An Account written by Laurence
Housman of his brother Alfred's Life . . . Deposited with the British Museum
Department of Manuscripts by Laurence Housman in May 1942.* London:
Little Rabbit Book Co., 1976. A biographical account, including extracts
from A. E. Housman's diaries.

Jebb, Keith. *A. E. Housman.* Mid Glamorgan: Seren Books, 1992. A recent critical study, offering a general account of Housman's work including poetry and prose.

Leavis, F. R. and Denys Thompson. *Culture and Environment*. 1933. Reprinted
London: Chatto and Windus, 1964. A critique of some developments in
modern civilization that are important for the literature of the period,
including changes from village life to urbanized and mechanized life, a
society dominated by advertisement, and the problem of widespread uni-
formity in minds as well as behavior. Published in the same year as
Housman's "The Name and Nature of Poetry," and written for specifically educational use, this work is an especially clear statement about the
conflicts in literary and intellectual culture which were important during
the years of Housman's maturity.

Leggett, B. J. *Housman's Land of Lost Content: A Critical Study of "A Shropshire
Lad."* Knoxville: University of Tennessee Press, 1970. One of the most
important book-length studies of Housman's poetry, this argument for
the unity of *A Shropshire Lad* has been influential.

———. *The Poetic Art of A. E. Housman*. Lincoln: University of Nebraska Press,
1978. On Housman's theory of poetry, examined in comparison with the
formal and artistic characteristics of his work and considered in connection with other important theories of the twentieth century, including
Freud's.

Lucretius. *On the Nature of the Universe (De rerum natura)*. Translated by R. E.
Latham. 1951. Reprinted Middlesex: Penguin, 1981. A philosophical
poem, and one of the most influential works of classical antiquity.

McGann, Jerome J. *A Critique of Modern Textual Criticism*. Chicago: University
of Chicago Press, 1983. An "argument for a socialized concept of author-
ship and textual authority" (p. 8) and one of the most influential contemporary arguments about textual criticism, a discipline which (with
classical scholarship) was Housman's profession.

———. *The Romantic Ideology*. Chicago: University of Chicago Press, 1983.
Influential argument that "one of the basic illusions of Romantic Ideology
is that only a poet and his works can transcend a corrupting appropria-
tion by 'the world' of politics and money" (p. 13).

———. *The Beauty of Inflections*. Oxford: Oxford University Press, 1985. Essays
on historical and textual criticism of nineteenth-century writers, showing
that interpretations *of* literature (no less than literature itself) are historically determined and historically variable.

———. *Social Values and Poetic Acts*. Cambridge, Mass.: Harvard University
Press, 1988. Essays on nineteenth-century and twentieth-century literary
works, especially in terms of their material and social relationships.

———. *Towards a Literature of Knowledge*. Chicago: University of Chicago Press,
1989. Essays on nineteenth-century and twentieth-century literary
works, concentrating chiefly on the "secret of the imagination" which is
"that it makes statements, that it communicates, that its architectonics
have designs upon us," including "meanings, designs, and purposes which
supervene the originary and authoritative ones" (pp. vii, x).

Mitchell, Sally, ed. *Victorian Britain: An Encyclopedia*. New York: Garland, 1988. A reference work including short articles on writers, events, concepts, and a broad range of topics.

Morgan, Kenneth O., ed. *The Oxford History of Britain*. Oxford: Oxford University Press, 1988. Includes "The Liberal Age (1851–1914)" by H. C. G. Matthew and "The Twentieth Century" by Kenneth O. Morgan.

Page, Norman. *A. E. Housman: A Critical Biography*. New York: Schocken, 1983. One of the most important biographies in recent decades.

Pater, Walter. *The Renaissance: Studies in Art and Poetry. The 1893 Text*. Edited by Donald L. Hill. Berkeley: University of California Press. One of the most influential books about art and poetry, and their relation to life, written in Housman's lifetime.

Pugh, John. *Bromsgrove and the Housmans*. Bromsgrove: The Housman Society, 1974. Important biographical information about Housman and other members of his family, including lawyers' correspondence concerning the financial dealings and misdealings of the poet's father.

Richards, Grant. *Housman 1897–1936*. London: Oxford University Press, 1941. A memoir, including 462 of Housman's letters. Richards was the publisher of the second edition (and later editions) of *A Shropshire Lad*, he published *Last Poems*, and he was Housman's friend for 40 years.

Ricks, Christopher, ed. *A. E. Housman: A Collection of Critical Essays*. Englewood Cliffs, NJ: Prentice-Hall, 1968. Reprints important essays including work by Edmund Wilson, W. H. Auden, Randall Jarrell, Cleanth Brooks, and others.

———. *The New Oxford Book of Victorian Verse*. Oxford: Oxford University Press, 1987. A good anthology of poetry of the period, recommended for students.

Russell, Bertrand. *Sceptical Essays*. 1956. Reprinted. London: Unwin, 1977. Philosophical essays written to be accessible to a general readership, by a former colleague of Housman's at Cambridge who lost his position there because of antiwar activities.

Sorley, Charles. *The Letters of Charles Sorley*. Cambridge: Cambridge University Press, 1919. Sorley was a poet who died during World War I. This work includes Sorley's paper on Housman.

Symons, Katharine E., et al. *Alfred Edward Housman*. Bromsgrove: Bromsgrove School, 1936. A collection of reminiscences of Housman by Katharine E. Symons (his sister), A. W. Pollard (a friend from his undergraduate days), Laurence Housman, R. W. Chambers (a student at University College London when Housman was professor of Latin there), Alan Ker, A. S. F. Gow, John Sparrow, and N. V. H. Symons. This volume was reprinted in the following year as *Alfred Edward Housman*. New York: Henry Holt & Co., 1937.

Weeks, Jeffrey. *Coming Out: Homosexual Politics in Britain, from the Nineteenth Century to the Present*. London: Quartet Books, 1977. An historical account, including information about Laurence Housman's work as chairman of the British Society for the Study of Sex Psychology.

Whittemore, Reed. *Pure Lives: The Early Biographers*. Baltimore: Johns Hopkins University Press, 1988. An account of the art of biography, showing how for earlier biographers (prior to Boswell) the public life was foremost.

———. *Whole Lives: Shapers of Modern Biography*. Baltimore: Johns Hopkins University Press, 1989. An argument about the art of biography, contrasting the modern academic tendency to accumulate detail (especially personal detail) with the more broadly social aims of great biographies of the past, and advocating greater attention to the ideological importance of writers' (and others') works.

———. *Six Literary Lives: The Shared Impiety of Adams, London, Sinclair, Williams, Dos Passos, and Tate*. Columbia: University of Missouri Press, 1993. Exemplary ideological biographies.

Index

The Author

Terence Allan Hoagwood, Professor of English at Texas A&M University, has taught previously at Vassar College, the University of Maryland, The American University, The Pennsylvania State University, and West Virginia University, where he was Benedum Distinguished Scholar in Arts and Humanities in 1986. Hoagwood is the author of previous studies of Housman's poetry and thought (in *Housman Society Journal* 1986, 1987, and 1988), and of scholarly articles on other writers and artists including Chaucer, Milton, William Godwin, Mary Hays, William Blake, James Gillray, Wordsworth, Byron, Shelley, Keats, Charles Kingsley, Gerard Manley Hopkins, Elinor Wylie, and Ellen Glasgow. His scholarly books include *Prophecy and the Philosophy of Mind: Traditions of Blake and Shelley* (1985), *Skepticism and Ideology: Shelley's Political Prose and Its Philosophical Context from Bacon to Marx* (1988), *Byron's Dialectic: Skepticism and the Critique of Culture* (1993), and *Politics, Philosophy, and the Production of Romantic Texts* (forthcoming from Northern Illinois University Press). He is also the author of a book of poems, *Secret Affinities* (1988), and he has published about fifty poems in journals and reviews. Hoagwood is the editor of several books, including Sir William Drummond's *Academical Questions* (1984), Drummond's *Philosophical Sketches of the Principles of Society and Government* (1986), Joseph Priestley's *Doctrines of Heathen Philosophy Compared With Those of Revelation* (1988), Mary Hays's *The Victim of Prejudice* (1990), Elizabeth Smith's *The Brethren* (1992), Charlotte Smith's *Beachy Head, With Other Poems* (1993), and Robert Stephen Hawker's *Cornish Ballads* (1994).